Enterprise Blockchain with Hyperledger®

An Introduction to Sawtooth™, Fabric™, Cello™, Composer™, and Hyperledger Explorer™

By

Mohammad Abdelalim

MOHAMMAD ABDELALIM

Enterprise Blockchain with Hyperledger

Copyright © 2019

ISBN: 9781700465337

Warning and Disclaimer

Publisher contact

Skinny Bottle Publishing

books@skinnybottle.com

To Amel Emara,

Since the first moments of my life, you focused on giving me a chance to learn everything, taught me to read newspapers at the age of 4 like an adult person does. Spent your savings entirely to provide me better education always. No words can be enough to thank you for being a loving mother and a good friend for more than 22 years.

About the Author

My Passion for the blockchain world started with an interest in cryptocurrencies and decentralization. as a non-experienced blockchain developer. I think that this book is a good chance to share knowledge as a learner, not as an experienced developer which I believe to be a better point of view for other newcomers to the blockchain world.

As most Egyptian Citizens did, I got much bureaucracy in my daily life. The bureaucracy itself is a result of centralization and I do personally believe that even the most advanced centralized technologies will fail before 2050. The movement toward a decentralized world is a not less important step than moving from papers to computers and I really hope that as much as possible people around this world understand the basics of blockchain technology to be ready for the changing future. Therefore, I hope that this book will be a little contribution to this beautiful future!

For any inquiry about the content of this book, or even if you want to discuss anything related, I'm always happy to respond to your emails at **abdelalim@grosware.com**

Chapter 1: Introducing Hyperledger

Getting to know Hyperledger and Blockchain

Trust.

How would a cave person trust another cave person while exchanging goods?

While humanity is moving forward, we found more ways to establish trust. We used real estate records, police records, etc. which we can call "Ledgers".

If you're coming from an accounting background then you probably know ledgers, but when it comes to blockchain - which we will be describing soon - we use the same term from a more general point of view.

I'd go with a very simple definition for a ledger

A Ledger is a collection of some related transactions saved into a storage model

A ledger might save data into any form, depending on the implemented algorithm for it, it might be into an actual database, some flat files, etc.

Anyway, these invented ledgers could establish more trust between a buyer and a seller while doing a transaction, so you could trust that your new home is in a good state, your new employee has no criminal record, etc.

But another issue started to show up, these ledgers are not fully trusted, someone can manipulate it in a way or another. Even for electronic records (or ledgers), someone can manipulate them and gain unauthorized access. We needed to have something better where both parties (the buyer and the seller) could agree 100% on a specific transaction, so we started to **decentralize** our ledgers, aka distributed ledgers. Distributed ledgers keep a copy of the same data into several different ledgers, a very common example is the Bit Torrent protocol, where everyone owns a copy of the same data, if someone changed the data they or another person is sharing, the protocol will be able to calculate the **checksum** of the data to know that someone did manipulate it.

A distributed ledger needs only three things to work efficiently:

1. A data model to keep the current data and state of the ledger.
2. A language or a procedure of transactions, which will be used to add new transactions.
3. A protocol to keep all ledgers in a group of distributed ledgers aware of any transaction.

Let's get back to commerce. In many areas, the transactions are kind of sequential, for example, let's imagine the transaction of buying the home number 123 ABC Street; the home was built in 1972 to be sold by the contractor in the same year to Mr. John Doe. The home was on fire in 1989, the house owned did refurbish the same year then he sold it to Mrs. Jane Smith in 1990.

Now you want to buy the home from Mrs. Jane Smith, how would you know that the house was on fire someday? Or in other words, how do we know that a transaction of type fire occurred on the house in 1989?

As all the transactions we discussed are related to the house, we can sort them into a chain of sequential actions, if we save these transactions into some blocks of data which are chained sequentially to each other, we can achieve a **blockchain** for the transactions we have.

Information saved into a blockchain depends on each other, and it is also saved into distributed ledgers. When we say it is dependent on each other we mean that if a certain record was modified (i.e. the fire record) the whole chain would be useless therefore it will be very easy to determine that something is missing as the whole ledger will be unreadable, Thanks to the implemented algorithms.

The Idea of blockchain was supported by some smart implementations of cryptography, which gives every block a hash pointer to the previous block! Which will make the whole blockchain unreadable if a single block was modified.

In 1990, Stuart Haber and W. Scott Stornetta published a revolutionary paper [1] on digital content time stamping, where they proposed the conceptual idea for blockchain to provide a timestamped and manipulate-proof way to store blocks of data.

This idea was later transformed into what we know today as Cryptocurrencies; to be specific it was **Bitcoin**. Bitcoin used an algorithm that ensured some powerful features never existed in normal money, I'll list the most important

1. Everyone can see the whole history of transactions!
2. All transactions are anonymous.

The first feature is the reason why you can never make a counterfeited bitcoin, simply because everybody on the planet can validate the history of the same bitcoin you're trading for a transaction! This feature never existed in a banking system, would the hairdresser call the Federal Reserve to validate numbers on the 10 dollars note you just gave to him? And even if he does so, and the federal reserve confirmed they issued these 10$ note, how would the hairdresser know he has the real 10$, and not a counterfeited copy with the same serial number?

With Bitcoin, like any other blockchain, you are not only checking the note itself, but you can also check that this bill is really owned by your customer and therefore it is a legitimate one.

The second feature is what makes cryptocurrencies in most cases different than any other blockchain transactions, so, you don't need any form of identity to create a wallet where you can keep your bitcoin despite that a normal user would need a software to make one.

These two features were revolutionary; they never existed in any currency system over history, and that's why Bitcoin prices are going viral in the time I am writing this book.

Blockchain made consensus between any parties involved in a transaction easier, but wait! What is consensus? From a language point of view, it is an agreement between some parties involved in something, the definition from a scientific point of view is more detailed, and there is a little issue that we should take care of.

Consensus Algorithms

Consensus is the process where two entities involved in a transaction can mutually understand, agree and execute this transaction. There are many algorithms for making consensus between entities, each of them is based on different requirements on both technology and business levels. Before we continue, let's get back to history.

The Byzantine Generals' Problem

More than a thousand years ago, a group of Byzantine generals, each one of them commanding a brigade of the Byzantine army, was circulating a city. And as expected the generals wanted to a good plan to attack the city. So basically, generals can do one of two operations, either Attack or Retreat, however, all generals must agree on one of the two operations, because it would be a massacre if only some of them decided to attack or to retreat. Generals agree by voting either they will attack or retreat.

As generals are circulating the city, each general can only communicate with two other generals and each of them can communicate with him and another general.

There is another issue, some of the generals might be traitors. Traitorous generals might cast a vote in favor of a bad action, but they can something more dangerous. Imagine that we have 7 generals, three voted in favor of attacking while three voted in favor of retreating. These 6 are loyal generals but the 7th is a traitor. The 7th one is responsible to pass votes to from the first three generals to the second three generals and vice versa, If he reversed the votes of each group before passing to the other one, the generals who wanted to retreat will attack and the generals who wanted to attack will retreat; with very basic military knowledge we can expect that the whole army will be slaughtered.

Now back to the blockchain industry. Most modern ledgers work with an assumption of Byzantine failure which will not be a traitorous general in this case, but probably an attacker or a kind of malicious software. Most algorithms need 3n+1 nodes to tolerate a Byzantine (bad) node (even if some algorithms need more). In most cases, there are other levels for validation along with enough nodes to correct any error.

But how can we avoid this failure from a technical point of view? There are two approaches to do so, and both require verification for votes. The first approach is known as the Nakamoto consensus which is used for Bitcoin mining. Using this approach, a leader is selected randomly and given the ability to add a block to the chain from a group of committed blocks by other entities.

When choosing a leader randomly, the randomization process has several things to take care of, they are:

1. Fairness: We should choose a leader from the widest possible group of entities involved in the distributed ledger.
2. Cost-Effectiveness: The process for choosing a leader should not cost too much compared to the value gained from it.
3. Verification: All parties should be able to validate the legitimacy of the process easily.

Several Algorithms maintain the three requirements above. They're so-called "Proof of Elapsed Time" and abbreviated PoET.

Note: In Bitcoin, the leader is the first entity to solve a cryptographic puzzle, and it can commit the mined bitcoin to the global blockchain.

The second approach is the traditional Byzantine Fault Tolerance (BFT) Algorithm. It simply uses more than one round of explicit votes to make sure that all votes were counted correctly. Several implementations were made for this approach.

Bitcoin was the first known implementation for blockchain, it was later followed by different implementations, either by more cryptocurrencies of some commercial transactions, but these implementations were based on the given algorithms, with no easy to use development framework that could make it easier for developers to create a blockchain-based application.

Despite a few small attempts to develop frameworks for the blockchain industry, there was no well-known framework at all, until Late 2015.

In December 2015, Linux Foundation announced a new... well, some people prefer to call it The Hyperledger Project, but I personally would see it as an umbrella of different projects. The Hyperledger Project is an Open-Source Project (You probably guessed it once you read Linux Foundation).

The best thing about Hyperledger is its wide range of supporters on enterprise-level, Hyperledger Project is supported by several tech companies and Independent Software Vendors (ISVs) including (but not limited to) Intel, Fujitsu, IBM, RedHat, Cisco, Digital Assets and Hitachi. When it comes to financing; the Hyperledger Project is also supported by J.P. Morgan, Wells Fargo, SWIFT, and Deutsche Börse.

There is also a governing board for the Hyperledger Project consists of 20 members from the contributing entities, they plan & organize efforts to improve the project.

So, what does Hyperledger provide? Hyperledger provides – At the time of writing this book – **Five Different frameworks** along with **Five Other tools**, the frameworks are:

1. Hyperledger Sawtooth
2. Hyperledger Iroha
3. Hyperledger Fabric
4. Hyperledger Burrow
5. Hyperledger Indy

And the tools are

1. Hyperledger Cello
2. Hyperledger Composer
3. Hyperledger Explorer
4. Hyperledger Quilt
5. Hyperledger Caliper

In the next few pages, we will go through a brief understanding of these Nine child-projects. This is just a brief introduction with information that is more business and architecture focused. The last chapters will be more focused on the development and code work itself.

Different Projects Under the Hyperledger Umbrella

Hyperledger Sawtooth

Hyperledger Sawtooth is (in my opinion) the most essential framework under the Hyperledger umbrella. It is used to build distributed ledgers which we described earlier. From a scientific point of view, the Hyperledger Official website defines a distributed ledger as

> *A distributed ledger is a set of communication protocols that enable administratively decentralized, replicated databases.*

Hyperledger Sawtooth is an enterprise solution, it doesn't only take care of the development process, but it is also used for deploying & running the distributed ledgers. Several Programming languages are supported, which are C++, Go, Java, JavaScript, and Python.

The most common usage for Hyperledger Sawtooth is through provided SDKs and REST API, this will be explained in later chapters of this book. Usually, a **transaction family** is made and associated with a business application that is using it (the transaction family).

But what is a transaction family? Transaction family is a group of transactions that are allowed on a specific ledger.

Each transaction family has a set of semantics for managing its transactions. Let's take a very basic example which is an integer key for some transactions in a family, we can only increment, decrement or set this integer key, but we cannot change its type from integer to a double for example, and we cannot delete it from a transaction too. Transaction families support, implemented into Hyperledger Sawtooth, is essential to prevent any intended or non-intended illegal transactions from missing with the blockchain which is very essential to prevent risks for any business.

Hyperledger Sawtooth can be used to build a transaction family from scratch. But it also provides several transaction families as models, they are:

1. Validator Registry: Provides a way to register ledgers-based services.
2. IntegerKey: Provides a way to test deployed ledgers.
3. Settings: Provides implementation for saving blockchain settings
4. Identity: Provides Identity and Permissions management on public keys for distributed ledgers.

Additionally, few other transaction families for specific fields are provided, they are:

1. Smallbank: Used for benchmarking the whole blockchain to know more about its performance. Implementation is based on the H-Store Smallbank benchmark.
2. Seth: This transaction family integrates with another project which is Hyperledger Burrow to support the creation and execution of smart contracts.
3. BlockInfo: Used to control how the transaction will be saved into blocks and the characteristics of each block. This one is essential for Seth smart contracts.

Some other transaction families are provided as implemented examples:

1. XO: Allow users to play Tic-Tac-Toe game (Also known as XO).
2. Supply Chain - Provides support for tracking physical objects in a real-world supply chain (check case study #1)
3. Track and Trade - Provides support for users to track items (either physical or logical) as they move through the supply chain, this includes information about items' history of ownership and history of other variables that related to the items itself.

Support is provided by Hyperledger Sawtooth for implementing, deploying and running distributed ledgers through modular design which provides dynamic and flexible ways to develop blockchain-based solutions with customized transaction families.

Like any other well-built framework, Hyperledger Sawtooth can be integrated with several other solutions including IoT (Internet of Things) and POS (Point of Sale) and anything else you can imagine.

A nice case study provided through the official Hyperledger website is about seafood from the sea to the table with blockchain. And Yes, this is a real case study where we can use Hyperledger Sawtooth and IoT to 100% assure legal & healthy fish on a dinner table.

I believe that case studies are the best way to explain something, so let's walk through a simplified version of this case study to ensure some basic understanding of Hyperledger Sawtooth.

Case Study 1: Seafood & Hyperledger Sawtooth

In nowadays fish supply chain industry, we're surrounded by several issues that impact both the business and consumer health. The most important four issues are the following:

Manually controlled records for fishing: Records for fishing and seafood packs are manually managed by employees on the ship.

Impact: Records are error-prone, it can be also counterfeited to cover fishing operations using explosives or any toxic substances (including cyanide sometimes).

Improper Seafood Storage Conditions: the seafood might be saved in containers or packs out of a refrigerator. It might also be exposed to sunlight and/or air for extra time due to the massive fishing operation that might exceed super refrigerator capacity.

Impact: Unhealthy seafood might be provided to consumers, causing severe health issues.

Seafood Mislabeling: either intentionally or non-intentionally, it happens every day that different types of seafood are mislabeled with other different types or different days of production and packing.

Impact: A lot of unsatisfied customers, which will make less revenue for the business.

So, let's take a minute to consider how can we solve this problem using Hyperledger Sawtooth and IoT.

Firstly, cheap IoT tags are available everywhere, they can be used to trace each pack of seafood as it is fished. But how can we make sure that data saved on these tags weren't counterfeited?

This is the turn for Hyperledger Sawtooth to group these data into a blockchain that can be viewed by all parties involved in this transaction. Including fishermen, traders, and consumers.

This can be achieved by following these steps:

1. Fish is Fished and physically tagged with IoT Tags.
2. Sensors on IoT Tags keep transmitted data about location and date for each pack.
3. Blockchain developed by Hyperledger Sawtooth keeps saving the data transmitted by these IoT devices.
4. Both Consumers and traders can access a comprehensive record about each pack to know everything about it.

Advantages achieved using Hyperledger Sawtooth

1. Trust established between buyer and seller while doing a transaction, the very same reason we developed blockchain in the first place.
2. Improved reputation for businesses using blockchain, which will result in better sales and customer satisfaction.
3. Saved effort and labor cost, no need for humans to record data about seafood packs.
4. In the long term, fewer health issues for consumers.

Before you started to read this weird case study, I guess you never believed that fishing industry is something that we can improve using Hyperledger technology, but here we are proving that whatever is the industry, whatever are the circumstances, we can build a reliable solution to improve it using blockchain technology. Seafood fishing is just a very complicated example when you look at it in the first place, but it is possible to be implemented easily in practice.

Hyperledger Iroha

Hyperledger Iroha is another framework to know about, it focuses on the incorporation with businesses that have infrastructural projects in need to be supported by blockchain technology. The official definition is

Hyperledger Iroha is a business blockchain framework designed to be simple and easy to incorporate into infrastructural projects requiring distributed ledger technology.

Iroha was incubated under the Hyperledger umbrella in November 2016, it was originally developed by Soramitsu which is a Japanese company and a Hyperledger member company. Soramitsu also committed several engineers on its workforce to maintain and update the project alongside with contributions that come from the Hyperledger community.

Iroha was inspired by the Hyperledger Fabric project architecture and it aims to complement both Hyperledger Fabric and Hyperledger Sawtooth projects by creating reusable components written in C++ but can be consumed within a variety of languages including Go and Java on Mobile, Web or Desktop environments.

The focus on making reusable components made Iroha an additive element to any project where blockchain technology is used with no need to make expensive changes to the business software itself. It was also built to complement Hyperledger Fabric, not to compete against it, so with a little background for Hyperledger Fabric; Any developer can write code for Iroha if they're a bit familiar with Hyperledger Fabric (and C++ too).

There are three main goals for Iroha, as listed on the Hyperledger blog post where Iroha release was announced, they are:

1. Provide an environment where C++ developers can contribute to the Hyperledger Project.

2. Make it easy to build infrastructure for Mobile and Web Applications.
3. Provide an environment to test new APIs and consensus algorithms which can be later added to Hyperledger Fabric.

These features made it easy for mobile & web developers (which takes most of the development market nowadays) to benefit from the blockchain revolution through easy to construct & use components empowered by the power and speed of C++ programming languages and supported by Sumeragi Algorithm. Sumeragi is a new powerful Byzantine fault tolerance consensus algorithm.

Iroha also provides (Via Sandbox JVM) a set of Turing-complete smart contracts. This means that you don't need to write chain code to define any digital asset, all you need to do is to consume the already provided code to start text messaging or to deploy a new cryptographic currency. This code is provided as a part of the Iroha core framework which is composed of the following sub frameworks

1. Iroha Core
2. Iroha Native iOS Library
3. Iroha JavaScript Library
4. Iroha Native Android Library

Iroha Core is designed to work on the distributed ledgers infrastructure to manage the membership services, consensus algorithms execution P2P network transmission and validation. Iroha Native iOS, JavaScript and Native Android Libraries are designed to make end-user activities like making and signing a transaction. Iroha can be integrated into other mobile platforms than Android and iOS through the Iroha JavaScript library if the target mobile device supports the modern web (Like Windows Phone or Tizen).

As we mentioned before, Hyperledger Iroha was made to complement two other projects (Hyperledger Sawtooth and Hyperledger Fabric), as a result; several components were made, and they can be reused for any other framework under the Hyperledger umbrella, these components are:

1. Sumeragi consensus library
2. Ed25519 digital signature library
3. SHA-3 hashing library
4. Iroha transaction serialization library
5. P2P broadcast library
6. API server library
7. iOS library
8. Android library
9. JavaScript library
10. Blockchain explorer/data visualization suite

Hyperledger Fabric

Hyperledger Fabric was originally developed by both Digital Asset and IBM, it was made as a foundation for developing modularly architected applications to make components like consensus algorithm validators and membership service providers to work with "Plug and Play" approach. This is essential when we're dealing with complex systems where there is no room for big changes in the source code, and more importantly, when we're linking more than one business together using the blockchain technology.

Hyperledger Fabric is like any other blockchain development framework, it has a ledger and a way to manage smart contracts, but the biggest difference is that Hyperledger Fabric is **private** and **permissioned**. It doesn't allow unknown identities to join the network. Other blockchain ledgers allow any entity to join the network after validation of Proof of work and other validation methods, but in Hyperledger Fabric the only way to join the ledger is by obtaining a membership from one or more **Membership Service Provider** (abbreviated **MSP**).

Membership Service Provider is a component or a module that aims to provide an abstract version of membership for nodes participating in a ledger. MSP doesn't care about protocols and procedures behind certifying a node, it rather focuses on the membership itself and its basic (or advanced) operations. Hyperledger Fabric ledger can be accessed through one or more MSP; to provide modularity for membership operations and interoperability across the network. You can also bring your own Membership provider service to any Project built with Hyperledger Fabric.

With Hyperledger Fabric, the data inside the ledger can be saved in almost all possible formats, also different consensus procedures can be added, switched on or off.

We mentioned before that Hyperledger Fabric can be used to build private and permissioned ledgers. Ledgers built with Hyperledger Fabric can be divided into different **channels**. Each channel can contain only a group of nodes participating in the ledger. To understand the reason behind that, let's imagine if we have 20 Companies working in the agricultural business, all these companies are required to participate in a ledger where they sell their products to the customer. But like any other business, the same product might be sold for different prices to different buyers depending on a variety of factors. Each company has a list of its most valuable customers, and of course, these customers can get some products at a lower price than other normal customers. Assumes that Company C_1 Sells the product P_1 to Buyer B_1 for 20$, but it sells the same product P_1 for other buyers for 25$, now Company C_2 Wants to gain Buyer B_1 from their competitor company C_1. Company C_2

Also provides Product P_1 for 22$ to all its customers. If company C_2 Knows the real price that company C_1 Provides to its Customers, they will be providing a discount for Buyer B_1 and sell the product for 19$ instead of 22$. But this won't happen, Why?

Because Company C_1 has created a channel on the ledger (which is built with Hyperledger Fabric) for its most valuable customers! And this channel is obviously private so that no competitors will be able to know the prices offered in the channel, even they will be able to know the public prices, they won't be able to access the private channel unless Company C_1 Adds them to it, which won't happen probably.

Hyperledger Fabric Docs Define a channel as:

> *A Hyperledger Fabric channel is a private "subnet" of communication between two or more specific network members, for the purpose of conducting private and confidential transactions.*

Hyperledger Fabric has a subsystem that comprises two components to keep track of transactions and nodes. The first one is **World State**, which is the state of the ledger at the current time and the database of the ledger, while the second one is the **Transaction Log**, which is the history of all transactions on the ledger which resulted in the current state, of course. All transactions are kept in order with respect to time regardless of the group or channel who committed it.

Hyperledger Burrow

Hyperledger Burrow is another framework used to build nodes to execute smart contracts based on the Ethereum specifications. Hyperledger Burrow was built to work with multiple blockchains while keeping optimization in mind to keep performance when integrating nodes built with Hyperledger Burrow with other applications.

Monax originally developed Hyperledger Burrow on December 2014 under the name ERIS-DB as an open-source project, but it was later supported by Intel and then incubated by The Hyperledger community in 2017.

Nodes built with Hyperledger Burrow are a bit complicated, so I believe the best way is to explain it as level, these Nodes are constructed based on 6 basic components, they are:

1. The Consensus Engine: keeps transactions in order and validates them using Tendermint protocol which is a good implementation for the Byzantine fault-tolerant algorithm. Tendermint provides high throughput for transactions and prevents the blockchain from forking (having different information on a different ledger, like the Byzantine problem).

2. Application Blockchain Interface: Also abbreviated as ABCI, is an interface for consuming the consensus engine. It isolates the smart contract application from the consensus engine.

3. Smart Contract Application: This is a transitional state between the ABCI and the Permissioned Ethereum Virtual Machine, where a transaction is validated once the consensus engine has finished work on it. It keeps all accounts and validator data. Accounts on Hyperledger Burrow have different permissions and can be authenticated either by a smart contract code or with public and private key encryption. When a transaction is made, the account code will be executed on the Permissioned Ethereum Virtual Machine.

4. The Permissioned Ethereum Virtual Machine: As we might have deduced from the previous point, This Virtual Machine is built to execute smart contract code. And it was built based on the Ethereum standards. It also asserts the permission to ensure that the right permissions are granted to the right participant.

5. Application Binary Interface: Also abbreviated as ABI, it transforms the transactions into a binary code that can be processed by the blockchain node. Provides functionality to compile, deploy and link smart contacts.

6. API Gateway: Hyperledger Burrow has a REST and JSON-RPC endpoints to ease the consumption of its features on different business systems while getting transaction broadcasting. Web Sockets are supported so that we can subscribe to events happening on the ledger.

Hyperledger Burrow is empowered with extra security that keeps in mind the future evolution. As Monax already had been involved in security before they announced the project, they secured the consensus cryptographically with Tendermint protocol. The better thing is that Tendermint was limited to accept cryptographic signatures from most validators only, using The Proof-Of-Stake mechanism which prevents unknown entities from getting into the consensus engine which might happen if we're using Proof of Work mechanism. Hyperledger Burrow accepts only the most cryptographic algorithms for remote signing. You can user ED25519/SHA512 or SECP256K1/SHA256 only (until the time of writing this book). Hyperledger Burrow connects to the remote signing service to generate Public and Private key pairs and to request signatures; this is also empowered by different technologies invented by Monax including Monax Keys.

Hyperledger Indy

Hyperledger Indy provides tools and reusable components for providing digital identities for distributed ledgers to unify these identities over different levels of the business applications and systems.

The project was incubated under the Hyperledger umbrella in May 2017, it is still in the development phases, but the initial versions are available for the public even before it was incubated by the Hyperledger Project.

The project was originally developed by Evernym, then it was gifted to Sovrin Foundation to support their efforts for building an open-source strong and reliable independent identity service on the Internet. In recent years, Sovrin Foundation built a global community of developers to help the world benefit from the economic and social that comes from Independent Identity being available widely.

But what is this Independent Identity We're talking about? Independent Identity makes every person, organization, or even a device able to obtain and own their own identity, not just controlling it.

For example, our personal email accounts are probably owned by an email service provider like Google or Outlook; even if it is on a personal domain the domain is still owned by a hosting service and we just have the right to "Manage" the account, not truly own it. So, email service or hosting service providers can simply pull out the plug and we can't do a thing (except some legal actions in some cases).

All these identities are soiled, not sovereign. Evernym tried (and succeeded so far) to provide a way through distributed ledgers technology for everyone to have their own self-sovereign identity.

Back to Hyperledger Indy; which implementation is not exactly Sovrin, but it is strongly associated with Sovrin to benefit from its perfect implementation.

So far Indy is under incubation, it is not yet released but as we mentioned before, the initial source code for Hyperledger Indy SDK and Node is available with limited documentation until the project is totally completed. The good news here is that Hyperledger Indy's SDK comes with wrappers for .NET, Java, Python and Swift (for iOS) which will make developers' jobs easier.

Now we're done with introducing the frameworks under the Hyperledger Project, but there are four tools remaining to introduce, they're also open source but they do supportive operations to the development of blockchain application, and not related to the development of the blockchain or the ledger itself.

Hyperledger Cello

Each blockchain has a lifecycle, this lifecycle consists of several activities like creating, managing and terminating a blockchain.

Hyperledger Cello aims to provide these activities with the as-a-service approach to reduce the effort needed by developers and DevOps people while managing a blockchain. Hyperledger Cello was designed to support blockchain lifecycle management on various types of infrastructure; such as virtual machines and container platforms.

The Approach Hyperledger Cello provides is called **Blockchain as a Service** (abbreviated BaaS). It focuses on improving the ability to provision blockchains instantly (for example Hyperledger Fabric) while tracking the overall system status to maintain the provisioned platform.

The project is architecture-neutral, it works on X86, POWER, Z and any other platform, Docker is also supported along with several other containers.

Hyperledger Cello uses a normal Master-Slave architecture, any node in the environment are either one of two things:

1. Master Node: which runs the Cello Service itself and can create or delete a blockchain and it comes either via a web dashboard or via a REST API.

2. Slave Node (The official documentation uses the term "Worker Node" instead): which holds the blockchain itself; as we mentioned before it might be a virtual machine or a container. The currently supported (in the time of writing this book) platforms are Docker, Swarm, Kubernetes, and vSphere.

Note: Slave nodes can be grouped into a host under one condition; all nodes in the same host must use the same resource controller (i.e. Docker or Swarm).

In an Interview with Jax Magazine earlier in 2017, Brian Behlendorf, the executive director of the Hyperledger Project pointed out that Hyperledger Cello is the start for **DevOps** in the Hyperledger Project, he said:

There is a broader issue that this domain is still very young, and we're still developing what you see in mature technology domains from a management and monitoring and design perspective — what you might call the "DevOps of blockchain". With the Cello project we are starting work in this space, the end goal of which is easy and fast deployment and management of the underlying layers so that everyone else can focus on smart contracts and apps on top.

DevOps is the process of unifying the Development process and the Operations related to the Development like provisioning virtual machines for testing for a very basic reason; Making the Software Lifecycle easier. Before we dive deep into code with Different Hyperledger Projects We will go through a dedicated chapter to explain DevOps concepts.

Hyperledger Composer

Company C is one of the most successful companies in the car rental business, they serve more than a thousand customers every day, thanks to their easy to use website which made listing and renting cars easier than writing a tweet. Their Chief Technology Officer (CTO), Mr. John Doe was looking to empower the business with blockchain technology so that car rental can be made through a distributed ledger. He could finally convince the management board to agree on that.

The Bad News: Using blockchain via CLI or other tools is easy for experienced computer users, but not for 99% of their customers, and moving the current data to the blockchain would cost a treasure.

The Good News: Hyperledger Composer is available.

Hyperledger composer allows you to model your business data into an existing (or new) business application.

The Project was launched in May 2017, it aims to extensively reduce the time needed for developing and deploying blockchain solutions from months to weeks. You can (After going into some steps) link your existing solutions to your blockchain to the end-users via the web using Node.JS But you still have to do a bit of work as you'll need to code another level between the blockchain and the web (even with some things already there). For General management of the blockchain itself and general information about it, we can use another project (Hyperledger Explorer) to have a nice ready to use dashboard.

So, in the case of Company C, they have

1. Cars: which we can call "Assets".
2. Car Owners and Car Renters: which we can call "Participants".
3. Activities for renting and listing cars: which we can call "Transactions"
4. Different things available for different users: which we can call "Access Control Rules" (abbreviated ACL).
5. Some Business-related functions: which we call "Transaction Functions", i.e. paying for rent.
6. Some predefined queries (probably for analytics): which we can call "Query Definitions"

How can we integrate these business elements into a blockchain? A Nice explanation is in this image:

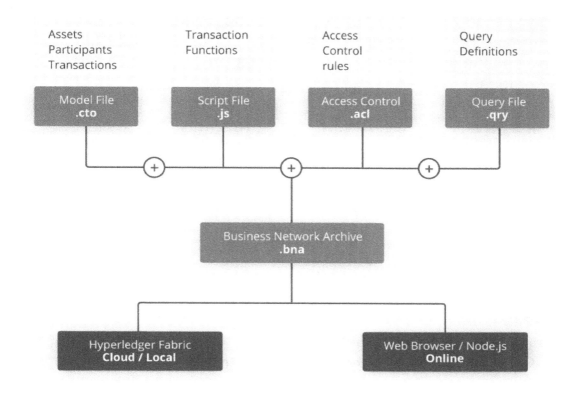

Source: https://hyperledger.github.io/composer/v0.19/introduction/introduction.html

Basically, with Hyperledger Composer, we will add all the business Participants, Assets and Transactions into one Model File (.CTO). This CTO File consists of a single namespace that implicitly contains all the business elements inside a set of resource definitions which will hold all the assets, participants and transactions.

The next step will be to define all the transaction functions into a normal JavaScript (.JS) file. Then we will add all the access control rules into an access control rule file (.ACL), and add all the query definitions into a query file (.QRY).

All these four elements describer (Model File, Transaction Functions, ACL and Queries) will be grouped with Hyperledger Composer into a single Business Network File (.BNA) which can be deployed to Hyperledger Fabric environment (Either on-premise or over the cloud); and can be accessed through web by consuming Node.JS functionalities provided by Hyperledger Composer.

Note: Hyperledger composer managed the connection between different elements using what is called Connection Profile. A Connection Profile is a JSON file that can be either saved as a file or as a system variable.

Hyperledger Explorer

Hyperledger Explorer is another module or tool that aims to make it easy to explore, query and invoke query blocks using a user-friendly web interface. Not to be confused with Composer; Composer is more integration and migration focused when we move an existing business to the blockchain technology. And building an application for end-users. Though Composer provides a gate to implement Node.JS applications on a blockchain, Hyperledger Explorer focuses more on making a general dashboard to ease management of the whole blockchain and providing some general statistics about it.

Hyperledger Composer gives an abstract way to access the business data on a blockchain that can be used later to implement interfaces for end-users, while Hyperledger Explorer focuses more on the Macro Management of the blockchain.

The Project was Originally an idea for an intern at Depository Trust & Clearing Corporation (DTCC) which was later discussed informally and got support from DTCC then it was incubated under the Hyperledger Umbrella. The Project is also known as Blockchain Explorer.

To build the needed environment for Hyperledger Explorer, we'll need Node.JS 6.9 (later versions are not supported) along with MySQL 5.7 (or higher).

Hyperledger Explorer is designed to work with Hyperledger Fabric 1.0. After preparing the environment for both Hyperledger Explorer and Hyperledger Fabric, we can access Explorer through a nice interface which immediately provides general details about the number of peers connected, the number of blocks, blocks list, next and previous hashes, number of transactions along with some graphs for quickly understanding the state of the blockchain.

Hyperledger Quilt

Hyperledger Quilt was incubated under the Hyperledger Umbrella in Mid 2017 after more than a year of research. Its mission is to provide connectivity between different distributed ledgers through Interledger Protocol (abbreviated ILP) To support payments between different ledgers. The project is incomplete until the time of writing this book.

The Interledger Protocol Project is maintained by the World Wide Web Consortium (W3C) and several other organizations and independent individuals. It was created to support secure payments between different ledgers as payments today are always soiled or disconnected. It also aims to protect payments between different ledgers from failures by isolating both the sender and receiver.

The Interledger Protocol is based on multi-hop payments and automated routing for transactions. It doesn't take care of anything except the functionality necessary for delivering a payment from source to destination. It doesn't include any support for public and private key pairs, identity, management or other services that are commonly provided in other payment protocols.

Let's get back to the Hyperledger Quilt which is an implementation for the Interledger Protocol in Java. And can be consumed through Interledger.js, both are hosted by Linux Foundation.

Hyperledger Caliper

Caliper is the most recent tool adopted in Hyperledger Family. it was announced on the 19th of March 2018 on the official Hyperledger project blog that Caliper was accepted by the technical steering committee under the Hyperledger Umbrella.

Hyperledger Caliper is a blockchain benchmarking tool which comes to support predefined test cases for blockchain implementation. which means that its user base consists of Software Developers, Testers and IT Pros. Blockchains implements a complex way to share data (consider hash calculation and Byzantine fault avoidance). hence, taking care of its performance is essential to maintain the business or community needs.

Before Caliper, there was no method to maintain a standard and neutral performance monitoring on blockchains. There are still few benchmarking tools made for few specific implementations of blockchains but none of them were generic to use with any blockchain implementation.

Hyperledger Caliper will generate readable reports contains information on Transaction per second (TPS), transaction latency, resource utilization, and other performance indicators. you can even customize it to have your own indicators and report views.

The Hyperledger Performance and Scalability Work Group (Appreciated Hyperledger PSWG) hopes that Hyperledger Caliper could solve the main three problems stated in its release blog post; these problems are:

1- Lake of open source code for the existing blockchain performance monitoring tools. Such a lake prevents the community from evaluating the efficiency and effectiveness of such tools.

2- Absence of definitions for performance indicators such as TPS, transaction latency, and resource utilization. An easy to deduce case is when a blockchain network is using smart contracts for its transactions; smart contracts execution requires more processing than normal transactions as it usually has higher complexity. When we calculate TPS for a network with smart contracts supported, we should take its complexity into consideration.

3- There are no commonly accepted use cases and scenarios for blockchain benchmarking. lake of commonly accepted use cases makes developers and decision-makers unable to understand the benchmarking itself and consequently in no possession to evaluate their implementations of blockchain.

From a Technical Point of view, Hyperledger Caliper can test several blockchain solutions integrated together. The secret behind this is the Adaptation Layer introduced in Hyperledger Caliper which allows integration of a single or multi-blockchain under test. For each blockchain, under test, a separated adaption model must be implemented. the model handles communication between Hyperledger Caliper NBI and the backend of the blockchain itself. At the time of writing these lines, Hyperledger Caliper supports the following blockchain projects (and Hyperledger Team is welcoming any more contributions for other blockchain systems.):

1- Hyperledger Iroha
2- Hyperledger Fabric
3- Hyperledger Sawtooth

However, The Hyperledger PSWG keeps it open and welcomes any help to expand Hyperledger Caliper to other blockchains.

Quick Recap

Now We have gone through a brief introduction for different projects under the Hyperledger Umbrella, and probably we have a bit of confusion between different projects under the umbrella. The best way to eliminate this confusion, in my opinion, is to give a few lines recap for each project in a quick list.

1. Hyperledger Sawtooth: Provides support for building, deploying and running distributed ledgers with a modular design. It is empowered by novel algorithms for consensus and Proof of Elapsed Time algorithms. It comes with a ready to use set of transaction families to speed up the development process.

2. Hyperledger Iroha: Provides support for C++ Developer to create reusable components easily with the support of its domain-driven and modern design which is empowered by C++. Hyperledger Iroha also features a new procedure for Byzantine Fault Tolerance.

3. Hyperledger Fabric: Provides support to build components (i.e. consensus engines or membership service providers) that can be used with plug and play approach. It supports building permissionable and private ledgers where a specific group of participants can communicate through a private channel, this is essential for many businesses to be able to move to the blockchain technology.

4. Hyperledger Burrow: Provide extensive support to build nodes that will execute smart contracts based on the Ethereum specifications. It is a permissionable smart contract engine built with specifications for Ethereum Virtual Machine.

5. Hyperledger Indy: Aims to provide totally independent identity to every person, organization or entity on the internet where everyone can "own" not just control their identity.

6. Hyperledger Cello: Brings normal blockchains into the Blockchain as a Service Model. It allows quick deployment of blockchains into different containers such as Docker, vSphere, Swarm and Kubernetes. Hyperledger Cello is the gate for DevOps and Hyperledger combination. DevOps will be introduced in the next chapters.

7. Hyperledger Composer: Provides support for integrating existing businesses into the blockchain technology after modeling the business data. It also provides a way to access the data with Node.JS technology so it can be implemented easily for end users.

8. Hyperledger Explorer: Provides an easy to use web interface for maintaining the whole blockchain by invoking or deploying blocks and getting overall statistics for the blockchain.

9. Hyperledger Quilt: Provides Support to make payments through different distributed ledgers.

10. Hyperledger Caliper: A Complete Benchmarking and reporting tool for blockchain networks. It has already implemented support for Hyperledger Iroha, Hyperledger Fabric and Hyperledger Sawtooth and can be expanded to any other blockchain network.

Case Study 2: Hyperledger and Company X

Company X is a leading company in the fresh food supply chain business. They provide mobile applications on three different platforms (Android, iOS, and Windows) which are developed using the Silo approach (each application is built natively for its platform) along with an easy-to-use website. Their business workflow is very simple, they make a connection between different types of customers and suppliers. Very simply, a customer who needs a specific amount of fresh food (more than 10 Kgs) will:

1. Sign up to the for an account (either with mobile or web application)

2. Verify phone number and payment method.

3. Browse a huge but easy-to-explore list of fresh food types available.

4. Click on a specific product.

5. The customer chooses whatever supplier from a list of suppliers who provide the selected product.

6. The Customer can see previous feedback on the supplier's public account.

7. The Customer specifies the amount needed of the product, with a minimum of 10 Kgs.

8. The Customer is contacted to verify the order and discuss price if needed.

9. The Price agreed is deducted from his preferred payment method along with a 3% commission for Company X.

10. The Requested product is delivered to the customer.

11. After 24 hours of the delivery, the customer will be prompted to write a feedback about the products he received.

So far everything seems to work perfectly, but there is an issue with the 6th step.

In many transactions, customers write strong negative feedback about food quality and freshness. In some cases, the customer can prove legally that he or she did receive low quality food, but in most cases when the food quality is bad, the customer will get rid of it and just write bad feedback.

Law in Country C (Where Company X headquarters are located) requires the deletion of any negative claim against businesses from servers located within the country if possible and as long as this claim can't be proven legally. This means that in most cases, company X will be forced to delete this negative feedback from its servers to avoid paying huge fines.

Company X has been dealing with this issue for a long time until their main competitor, Company Y, moved their small business into another country where laws are more tolerant in such cases. Customers started to abandon Company X platform and moving to Company Y to see true feedback on the products they're going to buy.

This issue made the management board curious about the decreasing curve of sales; few options were on the table including moving the whole business to another country, making every user sign an explicit disclaimer agreement. But Ms. Jane Doe, the smart young CTO researched extensively to find an outside the box solution, and she did.

As the law demands, the claims must be deleted if possible, but if the feedback can't be deleted then no one will be able to legally chase Company X!

To make feedbacks undeletable, the business must be moved to a blockchain running on a distributed ledger, there is not too much data to be kept on each ledger, so the storage won't be a problem.

In the next meeting Jane proposed the idea, there were some concerns about the migration progress, but Jane was prepared to answer all questions because of her good understanding of the Hyperledger.

The first concern was about the main ledger platform, should it be Hyperledger Fabric or Hyperledger Sawtooth?

Hyperledger Sawtooth Provides speed and low resource consumptions, but it doesn't provide private channels for communication.

Hyperledger Fabric Provides private transactions and great plug and play method which allows more dynamic control for it.

Of course, everyone prefers speed while dealing with high-speed transactions as the business grows and more customers and data will come, but the company provides a special program for the most important suppliers where they get fewer commissions paid from their side. Everyone agreed that the best option would be using Hyperledger Fabric, not Sawtooth.

Moving to other levels, there are several components used for the workflow, the components usually used to work through an API endpoint with PHP and MySQL backend. And these components need to be integrated into the new solution.

Previously, Company X choose PHP and MySQL to provide speed, but C++ can even provide fast processing too. And we can use Hyperledger Iroha to build modular and modern components with C++ to provide the same – or even better – performance compared to PHP. In Addition, using Hyperledger Iroha makes it a lot easier to integrate is with other components under the Hyperledger umbrella.

Also, there is a proposal to move the contracts from being centralized and traditional to be smart as it would make sense to have smart contracts with the Hyperledger based solution. Smart contracts can be provided easily with not too much coding effort with Hyperledger Burrow.

There is another issue going on, In Country A where some religious laws are being applied and Company X has several customers. Customers there need to obtain licenses to buy specific products and, in some cases, it might cause a lot of issues to obtain such a license. So, customers might prefer obtaining a kind of independent identity to obtain products which is a bit harder to be tracked by their government.

There was a discussion to integrate Hyperledger Indy within the project to help such customers but as the project is not mature enough yet and as it might cause other legal issues to Company X; the idea was postponed.

Another is point discussed was how to deploy all the nodes needed to establish a distributed ledger; It was agreed before that all suppliers would be required to install the new version of the application on their machine. Simply the new installer would create a vSphere environment empowered by Hyperledger Cello to run a copy of the ledger on each of the suppliers' machines. This way we can ensure that we will always have nodes running to host the ledger.

Another thing to care about is how can we migrate the existing data into the new distributed ledger? There are a few different user rules, a huge history of transactions along with different business functionalities.

Hyperledger Composer has the answer, as we discussed before it is totally easier to migrate the old data within few weeks along with all Access Control Rules and business functionality plus the existing queries used by the business analysis team in company X.

Another issue solved by Hyperledger Composer was providing a communication channel between the distributed ledger and the end-user applications, as we mentioned before there are four different applications; web, Android, iOS and Windows Phone. Jane firstly thought about the effort needed to change these applications. It wasn't hard as it can be supported directly by Node.JS which is already provided by Hyperledger Composer. For mobile applications, Jane firstly thought about changing the data models in each of the three to read from the same API consumed by the web application, but it was costly to change the code in the three applications.

For a moment, Jane wished there is a way to change all of them together without having to re-write most of the code again. Then another idea was in her mind! If Hyperledger Composer provides the Node.JS interface, why not go for a cross-platform environment like ionic which is also empowered by Node.JS and has a single application that runs on several platforms?

This could even reduce the future cost of maintaining the application and also deliver the same experience for all users. The idea was accepted which took development cost for mobile applications 50% down.

For maintaining the blockchain itself, Hyperledger Explorer could provide help. Jane can check-in any time (and even create alerts) if the number of nodes running is going below the number needed to run the network efficiently from one rich webpage. If for a miracle there were few nodes on the network, Jane can quickly deploy another node to any cloud service until enough nodes are back to work.

Also, if needed in future, any supplier in this case study who's willing to buy fresh seafood from fishermen in case study #1 can depend on the future integration of Hyperledger Quilt to directly fund their purchases from the revenue coming from Company X's platform, but it is too early to think about that as Hyperledger Quilt is still a dormant project.

Chapter 2: Introducing DevOps

What is DevOps?

In the first few decades after the invention of computers, developing new software wasn't as hard as nowadays. You might disagree with this phrase, but I think that there are two points of view to consider.

1. How is it easy to write the code itself? What is the availability of different knowledge sources? can we find books and tutorials easily? what are the limitations that keep our dreams from becoming a real-world software solution?

2. How is it easy to make sure that the developed code can work on different platforms under different conditions, how many different platforms we must support?

For the first point, I believe it is easier now. For any programming language or technology, you can imagine there many tutorials and documentation available in free in most cases.

For the second point, I believe it is harder now. Because in the old days there were not many platforms and environments as we have now.

In General, we can see the development lifecycle into nine steps

1. **Planning**: What are you going to do?

2. **Code**: Write the source code for the application.

3. **Build**: Convert your code into something that can run.

4. **Test**: Make sure you've built the right thing in the right way.

5. **Release**: Take what you've tested out of development labs.

6. **Deploy**: But it in the right environment and run it.

7. **Operate**: Get the benefit you developed the software for in the first place.

8. **Monitor**: Keep tracking performance and other benefits you expected, are you getting as expected or not?

9. Go to step 1 and carry results from step 9 with you.

The first four steps are **Development** Related.

The next four steps are **Operations** Related

The ninth step is just for your business survival.

Development and Operating Developed software are the main steps for any technology or application to succeed.

The Term **DevOps** Was coined from **Dev**elopment and **Op**eration**s** that follows development.

DevOps is a big concept to digest in a few lines. It aims to make the software lifecycle automated and robust as much possible by instating agility best practices in the team, the process and the product being built itself.

Case Study 3: Company M's infinite loop

Company M is a software development company. Most of their deals come as outsourced development projects from other companies that can't invest heavily in their own development departments.

Company M has a business team that is responsible to collect requirements and business-related communication, another team is the development team which is responsible for programming the requirements.

Another team is responsible for testing the project in different environments to make sure of its reliability on different platforms.

There another "Deployment and follow up team" which is responsible for deploying solutions and getting feedback from customers and sending it to the requirements team again.

The process seems to be very simple and straight forward, but a deep look inside will expose the truth. Let's take an example when Company S requested that Company X develops a new mobile application for its fashion business. As usual, the business team made several business meetings to initiate the project, the requirements were passed to the development team to create a very simple prototype of the application.

After several reviews and some communication efforts, the prototype was accepted, and the real development started. After the team made the beta version of the application they sent it to the business team to be shared with Company S.

Company S requested some minor modifications that were passed back to the business team to be forwarded to the development team (Too much effort on communication going on). Developers started to share the code in development through the network and storage servers, which caused a lot of confusion between developers about different internally used versions of code.

Consequently, the development team passed what they have made to the testing team. The testing team checks the application on several other levels alongside the business requirements (i.e. code readability and performance). They have to check the output of each function manually to make sure of its performance and correctness. Then testing each class or module in general. They have found some sever issues and contacted the development team back to ask for fixes to it. The Testers felt like the development team is throwing their work over the wall to the testing team which isn't healthy for the work environment in the long term.

Anyway, the development team made the work requested and sent it back to the testing team.

Testing team (After finishing internal check) moved to check if the application works on all supported mobiles or not. The application is built with Java to run on Android devices; therefore, the application must be tested on a wide range of android devices to ensure its reliability for customers.

The responsible Tester must test the application on hundreds of different platforms, previously this was done manually, but later it was semi-automated with a management tool. However, as the number of devices must be supported is increasing; the tool has been inefficient as it takes much time to test and, in many cases, it gets interrupted.

The process totally seems like trying to run a modern application on a Turing Machine from the 1950s. It causes the service level agreement for Company M to increase over time until it made the whole company to be a bad choice for any business. Competitors for company M gained more customers as they try to apply the best practices for DevOps.

As we mentioned before, DevOps improves the software development lifecycle at all by enforcing the real agility as it should be.

Let's walk through all the issues that happened to Company M.

1. The exhausting communication effort: According to modern agile practices, all stakeholders should be involved during the development lifecycle. This removes the overload on the business team who works as a messenger between different teams and the business itself.
   We can achieve this by using a modern solution to integrate all efforts by different stakeholders, several solutions for that are available either over the cloud or on-premise (i.e. Trello, Team Foundation Server, Visual Studio Team Services) where work is divided vertically (by amount) and horizontally (by type) and all stakeholders can provide on-time feedback on almost everything. Very basically the work is made publicly between all the stakeholders. **Can we relate this to the transparency gained by Hyperledger?**

2. The difficulty to locate different versions of the source code: This can be achieved through using a modern source control solution. Sharing files and using old fashioned tools like SVN is no longer reliable. Everyone is going for Git. Several solutions that provide simple and easy to learn interfaces for Git (i.e. Team Foundation Server and the most famous one, GitHub).

3. The effort needed to transfer work between teams: using the same solutions we mentioned before to solve communication issues (i.e. Trello, Team Foundation Server, Visual Studio Team Services) makes it easy to transfer work between different teams as it easy to drag and drop and item, literally.

4. The manual testing process: almost every programming language or development platform has its own unit testing tools that can re-run the tests again on every new version of the application, this is also called Smoke Testing.

5. The inefficient tool to manage testing on different platforms: Different tools were built to solve this issue; modern solutions use virtualization to solve this issue by deploying copies from different platforms on several virtual machines (each of which is dedicated to one platform).
Also, all the virtual machines are managed through a single tool; several tools can achieve this goal including Microsoft Hypervisor or the wide range of tools provided by VMWare and Oracle.

Moving to DevOps

Transitioning an existing software development lifecycle into DevOps costs a lot of money, but this can't be compared to the gains achieved. But the hardest thing is to transition team (**People**) itself to accept agility as it should be. People go always against changes. Nobody will encourage changes as the comfort zone is always preferred. But this preparation must be made increasingly as the transformation is going on for the technologies.

The next thing to transit is the **Process** itself if we have the most modern technology with bureaucratic procedures it would become useless. The new technologies are made to accommodate new enhanced processes, but if the tools were accommodated to the old inefficient process, the only thing gained will be a negative amount of money.

The last thing to transit is **Technology**, each company has its own business workflow and team. Tools should be selected based on various reasons, but the most important thing is to transit people first as we mentioned before.

More advanced topics in DevOps include **Continuous Integration** which focuses on continuously integrate work done by individual developers into the main repository. Also, **Continuous Deployment** which is also an extension for continuous integration but aims to continuously deploy new code to the production environment while giving developers confidence that their new code won't cause issues.

Another Technology is the **Continuous Delivery**, Continuous Delivery aims to ease deploying new code to the application used by end-users. Basically, Developers can schedule build time and deployment time to publish application finally to the end-users. The technology went wild that you can even take a snapshot from the source code on a specific day of each week or month, build it and automatically deliver and publish the new application to the end-users automatically without human intervention at all.

Chapter 3: Hyperledger Sawtooth

In the first chapter of this book, we introduced Hyperledger Sawtooth quickly from a business point of view with a little bit of tech talk. In this chapter, we're going to Dive Deep into code stuff through five laps. However, It is strongly recommended to read the introduction before proceeding to the dive deep tutorials.

Development with Hyperledger Sawtooth is either Application Development or Core Development or the Solidity Development (which is the development made to transactions and events itself). As everyone could guess, if you're developing an end-user application it is considered to be Application Development, and we're doing core development if we're customizing the core itself to match some business needs.

Understanding Sawtooth Architecture

Before Diving Deep into Sawtooth Development, let's review the project architecture quickly as we will depend on it to understand the different possible roles for each developer on a Hyperledger Sawtooth environment.

Global State

It is the main goal for any distributed ledger to maintain the same state for all nodes participating in the ledger. Achieving such a result needs a lot of effort to be done; Thanks to **Merkle Tree** Implementation within Hyperledger Sawtooth.

Merkle Tree (AKA Hash Tree) is a data structure originally patented by Ralph Merkle (who is known for the invention of cryptographic hashing and contributions for public-key encryption).

In any Merkle Tree, each leaf node is a block of data, and each node that is a parent for other nodes (non-leaf) is a cryptographic hash to its children.

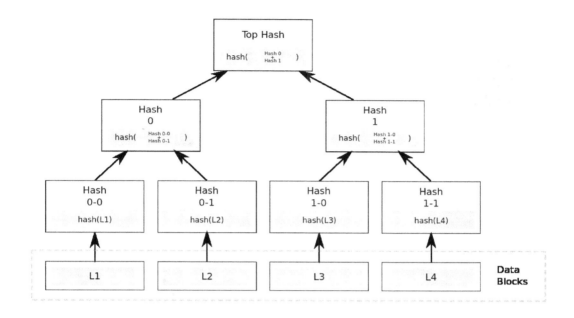

Source: https://en.wikipedia.org/wiki

Verifying that a leaf belongs to the hash tree takes log(n) of the leaf nodes count in the tree; therefore, Merkle Trees provides a reliable method to check very large hash files.

Once we add a new transaction, all nodes pointing to the leaf which holds the data for this transaction will be updated (AKA the branch pointing to this leaf will be updated).

Merkle Tree is already everywhere around us if you haven't noticed yet; it exists in Bit Torrent protocol, Bitcoin, Ethereum, Git and Apache Cassandra.

The Implementation for Merkle Trees in Hyperledger Sawtooth is also **Addressable Radix Tree** Implementation. In Radix Trees each node that is the only child is merged with its parent node. This will result in the number of children for internal nodes is at least the radix of the tree itself which is a positive integer and a power of the number two. This leads to a storage-optimized tree than regular trees.

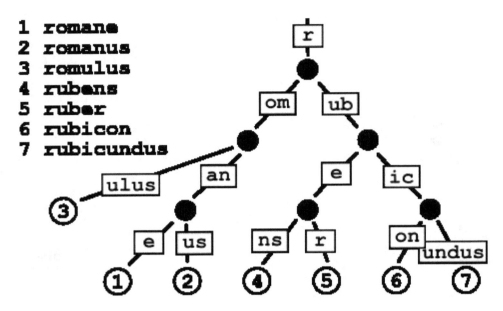

1 romane
2 romanus
3 romulus
4 rubens
5 ruber
6 rubicon
7 rubicundus

Source: https://commons.wikimedia.org/wiki

Each address in the tree implementation is 35 bytes represented by a 70 characters hexadecimal address. Three bytes are used to determine namespaces within an instance of Hyperledger Sawtooth, this gives us 6 hexadecimal characters with 2^{24} possible namespaces inside the instance. The remaining 32 bytes (64 hexadecimal character) are designed based on other specifications like object types classification or mapping unique identifiers for the business itself.

Further Step is the data **Serialization** and **Deserialization**. Serialization is the process of transforming data into a form that can be saved into storage (i.e. Binary format), while Deserialization is the process of transforming data from storage format into a usable format.

In Hyperledger Sawtooth, Namespace designers should define the serialization and deserialization processes for data stored in a specific address. The Transaction Processor makes two functional calls to the current state of the ledger provided by the validator.

The first function is get(address) which returns an array of bytes for data in the given address, while the second function is set(address, data) which sets data in the given address. It is very important to choose a serialization scheme that is deterministic for all transactions' executions on all platforms. It is strongly recommended to use data structures where ordered serialization is maintained because if the data was serialized in different order; then the outputted data array will differ between different nodes; causing some validators to accept a transaction while other transactions might not, which is considered as ambiguous behavior (Can you relate that to the Byzantine Generals Problem?).

Transactions

Transactions made to Hyperledger Sawtooth are grouped into Batches. Batches (when sent to the validator) are either all accepted or all non-accepted (i.e. the validator will never accept some transactions within a batch and reject others). i.   Then one the validator applies the accepted batch (if any) the state will be changed.

Each Batch consists of a set of transactions, the batch header, and its (the batch) signature. Each

Transaction consists of its header, payload and header signature which is signed by the transaction maker's private key and will be used to verify the transaction later when the whole batch is processed.

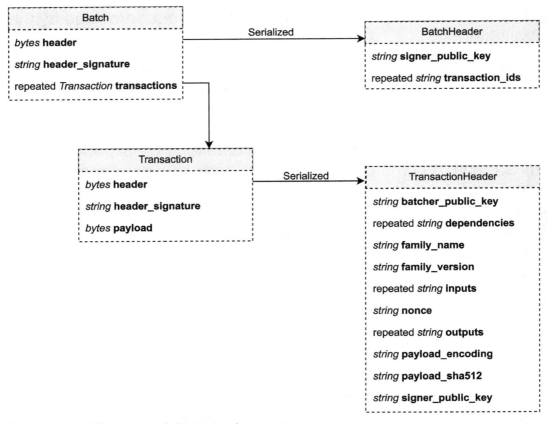

Source: https://github.com/hyperledger/sawtooth-core

Grouping transactions into batches overcomes many dependency issues; a clear example is when we have several transactions in a dependency circle (i.e. their dependency is iterative) And of course, the dependency in Hyperledger Sawtooth is ordered, therefore a transaction cannot depend on a transaction that will occur later (which will make extra constraints for businesses using blockchain technology). But with Batches, we validate and accept these transactions together without issue in a single batch.

It is also very important to point that batches are transaction family heterogenous. You can group transactions from several transaction families into one single batch. For example, we can group a money transaction with an identity verification transaction in the same batch.

> *Note: each transaction must contain the public key of its batch signer in the batcher_pubkey field to assure one batch for each transaction (Relation between batch and transaction must be one to many).*

Other Thing to take care of is Transactions Scheduling, Hyperledger Sawtooth allows both options; parallel and serial scheduling. This can be specified either via CLI or as an option specified by the developer in the Validator configuration file. The same result is always generated despite the scheduling method (serial or parallel used). However, there is a case when we shall prefer one over the other; As you might have already guessed, Parallel Scheduling is better when we want faster transaction processing but will consume a higher amount of computational power. On the other side, serial processing is better when we have hardware limitations.

Journal

As you might have guessed from the name, Journal is responsible for adding new blocks to the blockchain and doing the necessary validation for them. The Journal uses batches and blocks that arrive at the validator, and it consists of several components.

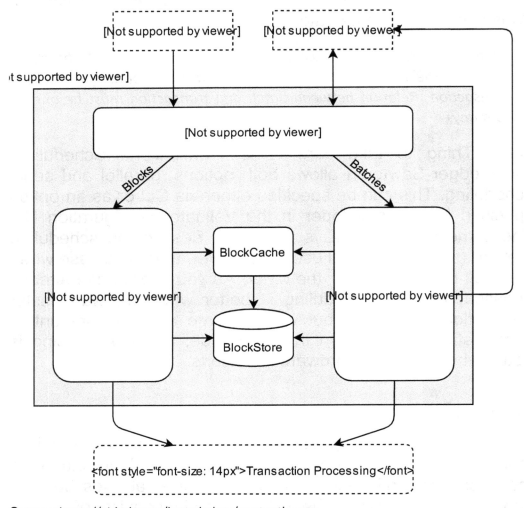

Source: https://github.com/hyperledger/sawtooth-core

The First component to talk about it the **Block Store;** Block Store is the place where all valid blocks are saved forever. It keeps all the blocks from the Genesis Block (The Oldest or Initial block in the blockchain) to the Chain Head (The most recently inserted block in the blockchain).

Errors in Block Store might be Bad Indexes, corrupted or missing blocks or invalid chain references; However, any error in the Block Store is non-recoverable for the validator. Good implementation of Hyperledger Sawtooth will prevent any errors anyway.

All Blocks within Block Store are complete blocks and can be accessed by Block Id directly or by Batch and Transaction Id Indirectly through some implemented functions like GetBlockByTransactionId and GetBlockByBatchId. Mapping between Blocks, Batches, and Transactions are maintained also by Block Store. If any error occurred to this mapping it will be checked and rebuilt on the next system startup and not during the runtime. It is also important to know that mapping isn't required to persist in the memory all the time, it will usually be retrieved from disk when needed.

The Second component is **Block Cache** which is the temporary memory for the validator. It keeps track of processing state for blocks being processed for the validator. Processing state is either valid (verified by the Chain Controller, we will explain Chain Controller a few lines later), invalid (failed validation or precedes an invalid block) or unknown which has not yet passed or failed validation.

The Third component is The **Completer**, Completer has a simple task which is to check that all blocks and batches being delivered are complete (i.e. their predecessors were delivered to the Chain Controller). Batches can be considered complete if all their dependencies are met.

The Fourth (and big) component is the **Consensus Interface**, Consensus Interface is responsible for applying consensus algorithms suitable for the blockchain initially (in it can be changed later). Three internal interfaces are there within the consensus interface; they are:

1. **Block Publisher**: Block Publisher creates new possible blocks from batches it receives from nodes as candidate blocks to extend the chain. Firstly, the Block Publisher initializes the block immediately after the block header is

initialized, then it checks (based on the in-use consensus algorithm) if the header is correct; this step is contained within the event *initialize_block*. The second step is to check if the block can be published, this is done either by polling or by validating if the wait time was expired (in case of using Proof of Elapsed Time PoET method), this step is applied through event *check_publish_block*. The last step is to finalize the block, the block published marks is block header as complete, waiting for the consensus fields to be filled, once done, the block is signed by the Block Publisher and shared within the network to other nodes, this is done within event *finalize_block*.

2. **Block Verifier**: This interface allows consensus algorithms to validate that the block being published is following the consensus standards applied in the blockchain.

3. **Fork Resolver**: If you're familiar with the fork concept in Source Control or DevOps, then you probably have guessed what fork means when it comes to blockchain technology, and you're almost right. Fork Resolver is responsible for assigning the valid block to the next.

The Fifth component is the **Chain Controller**. Chain Controller is pointing to the chain head (The last block in a blockchain is called Chain Head). This is essential for the fork resolver to apply its previously taken decision. Upon adding a new possible block, the chain controller will do the math to calculate the new state and Merkle hash for the new block, if valid, the Chain controller will point to the new block (As it will be the latest block).

A good map to explain the work of Chain Controller, Block Validator, Block Publisher and Fork Resolver is shown below.

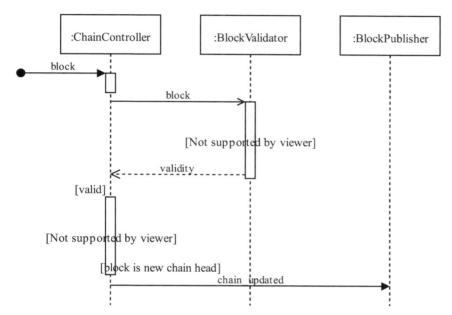

Source: https://github.com/hyperledger/sawtooth-core

REST API

Hyperledger Sawtooth Was initially built to make it easier to develop blockchain applications and transform the original paper published by Satoshi Nakamoto into something that modern developers can use to build great applications. For this reason; Hyperledger Sawtooth Provides a Restful API between the validator and clients that can be consumed in the most known format by Developers nowadays; It is JSON over HTTP. The API is isolated as the validator is treated like a separated module, and API is language independent.

The API documentation follows the OpenAPI specifications (Previously named Swagger), all aspects of the Hyperledger

Sawtooth API are documented with great attention to details in YAML format which can be accessed from the Hyperledger Sawtooth GitHub Repository.

For the sake of simplicity, not all HTTP status codes are included within the API (Actually not all of them are needed). Here is a list of the supported status codes:

HTTP Response Status Code	Meaning
200	OK
201	CREATED
202	ACCEPTED
400	BAD REQUEST
404	NOT FOUND (Even Non-Developers Know It)
500	INTERNAL VALIDATOR OR API ERROR
503	VALIDATOR SERVICE UNAVAILABLE

Note: Hyperledger Sawtooth API doesn't support authorization until the time of writing this book, but this is expected to be developed in the future; however, it is still possible to add some programmatic authorization beside the API usage.

There are Six Parameters that can be sent to the API, they are:

1. **head:** Specifies the id of the block that will be used as the chain head for the blocks within the response. Not to be confused with the chain head for the whole block, we mean the chain head for the response itself here.

2. **count:** Paging related, used to specify the number of resources needed, if not sent within the request, the default value will be *1000*.

3. **min:** Paging related, used to specify the id of the index first block to be retrieved, if not sent within the request, the default value will be *0*.

4. **max:** Paging related, specify the id or the index of the last block to be retrieved.

   Note: You cannot use the max parameter with the min parameter in the same request; therefore, if not specified the default for min parameter will be sent (which is 0).

5. **sort:** Used to sort the list of resources returned by the API, all we need to do is to pass the parameter with the key that the list will be sorted with, nested keys within resources are also supported through dot separator.

6. **wait:** Used to specify wait time for the API to response, accepts any positive integer as a value, if not specified the value will be determined based on the API's available time slot.

Example 1:

http://HyperledgerAPI.domain.com/blocks?count=100&min=200&sort=header.signer_pubkey

In this example, the count parameter specifies that we need only 100 blocks to be returned, the min parameter specifies that we need to start from the block number 200 and finally, the sort parameter orders that all blocks should be ordered by signer's public key which is included in each block's header.

Example 2:

http://HyperledgerAPI.domain.com/blocks?head=343&max=500&wait=5

In this example, the head is set to the block number 343, with maximum 500 blocks to be retrieved and wait time of 5 seconds (not milliseconds)

There are other four possible simple returned parameters from API, they are:

1. **data:** The actual resources returned from the blockchain.
2. **head:** Id of the first resource returned.
3. **Link:** A Hyperlink to the same resource returned.
4. **paging:** Specified how the returned data were paged.

If any errors occurred, an error parameter will be returned, and it will contain other three response parameters inside of it, they are:

1. **code:** contains an integer value indicating the error code as per the previous response table.
2. **title:** contains the error title.
3. **message:** contains the detailed message description of the error.

Validators' Communication, Permissioning, and Events

Validators in each participating node need to establish communication between them to agree on different actions they take on the blockchain. This is achieved through the network layer, this is referred to within official documentation as "Validators Network" which handles many activities including peer discovery and initializing the connection.

One of the essential rules specified was that we should isolate the network as much as possible, the network shouldn't need any knowledge of the message's payload to move it. For this purpose, Hyperledger Sawtooth's network uses the widely known 0MQ Client Server Network Pattern. The Pattern consists of a Router Socket on the server-side that listens to the endpoint (within the server). On the other side, Other Dealers are connected to the server (as clients). The client connects to a server and sends requests, the server (which is a peer and in another case will be another client) will either respond with 0 (no reply) or few replies, the server also can send several other replies without waiting for more requests.

The connection between any two validators will have one of possible three states, either unconnected (default), connected or peered. The connected state is a step between peered and unconnected states and messages cannot be passed if the state hasn't peered.

When it comes to Permissioning, two groups of Permissioning are mainly available; the first one is transactor based, called "Transactor Key Permissioning" which controls transactions and batches acceptance based on signing's key. The second group is validator based, called "Validator Key Permissioning" which checks and controls if a validator can join the validators' network or not.

Though not needed in many cases, Hyperledger Sawtooth Supports Implementation of Additional Events. The Term "Event" may refer to blockchain-related events (such as a new block being added to the chain or a block didn't pass through the Block Verifier) or application-specific events that might be defined within the transaction family. A further explanation for custom events can be found on Hyperledger Sawtooth documentation.

Getting into Core Development

These are simple steps to get into Developing Core Development for Hyperledger Sawtooth. Tools used in this tutorial are available for Linux, Windows, and macOS.

Preparing Environment

To avoid several system issues that might occur, we're going to use the power of virtualization and built the environment over a virtual machine easily deployed by Vagrant and VirtualBox.

Exactly, we need to install both Vagrant (v 1.9 or higher) and Oracle VirtualBox (V 5.1.16 or later). Also, Git should be there to clone the repository, so if you are using windows then download Git for Windows (any version would do the work).

Vagrant is an easy to use tool used to build and control virtual machine environments from one place. It focuses on isolating dependencies in a single consistent environment while allowing other development tools and applications to be included within the environment. Needless to say, it is environment independent.

Hyperledger Sawtooth repository on GitHub contains ready to use Vagrant configuration files within its dev tools directory "sawtooth-core/tools". These files make it a lot easier to start the environment in a few minutes.

Initially, we need to clone the repository locally, run the following command (after navigating to the desired directory):

```
git clone
https://github.com/hyperledger/sawtooth-
core.git
```

Inside the cloned repository, there are several files to talk about:

1. **bootstrap.d** directory: contains some bash scripts that will be executed during virtual machine provisioning once "vagrant up" command is executed.

2. **guest-files** directory: other files used by the bootstrap.d scripts also contain a script (local-env.sh) that contains some environment variables.

3. **plugins** directory: contains pluggable scripts that can be executed during provisioning but after bootstrap.d script.

4. **Vagrantfile** file: contains main configurations for Vagrant. Written in ruby and executed every time we run "vagrant up" command.

5. **package_groups** directory: contains dependency information for Docker, Latex, and Ubuntu.

If your network is relying on a proxy to connect for some reason, you can enable proxies within Vagrant by adding environment the following environment variables And Vagrant will automatically detect the settings.

1. http_proxy
2. https_proxy

Turning the Engine On

Navigate to /tools directory with your command line, then type

```
vagrant up
```

This step might take several minutes depending on your machine performance, once completed, type

```
vagrant ssh
```

Vagrant will create a user named vagrant with a user id (uid) 1000 by default, this newly created user has full administrative privileges on the virtual machine and can execute commands with no need for a password. The last command will establish an SSH connection to the machine (authenticated as default vagrant user).

To build the environment navigate (with the same command line) to /bin folder, type:

```
build_all
```

This will build the application, to run initial tests (just to make sure we didn't miss anything), within the same folder (/bin), type

```
run_tests
```

In case of any issues, the most recommended thing to go is to ask the community through one of several available communication channels available online, these channels can be accessed through the online website for Hyperledger Sawtooth (Hyperledger.org)

Chapter 4: Hyperledger Fabric Deep Dive

Both Hyperledger Sawtooth and Fabric Provides Means to develop Blockchain solutions, but Hyperledger Fabric provides more modularity and enterprise solutions focus. We will try to explore as much as possible for Hyperledger Fabric as it has been a good trend in the blockchain industry.

Something we should define initially before proceeding is the chain code. **Chaincode** is a program written in Go Programming language and sometimes in other programming languages like Java. Chaincode runs in a secure Docker container which is isolated from any other processes running on the peer environment. Chaincode initializes and manages distributed ledgers state when different transactions are submitted by peers. Chaincode transforms logic commands between different nodes into what is known as smart contracts. In the documentation we will find two different perspectives to understand Chaincode, the first one is from the operators' perspective while the second one is from the developers' perspective. We can divide the developers' point of view into two separate other points of view, one for Core Developers while the other is for Application Developers.

Key Elements of Hyperledger Fabric Environment

The Official Documentation for Hyperledger Fabric (which is written and maintained by the community) made a great division of Hyperledger Fabric into Six elements, this division is not so technical, but it aims to prepare the reader's mind to understand the deep technicality without confusion. The elements are:

1. Assets: Assets are anything that might be sold with a price, it can be a physical thing (A fish or a car) or nonphysical (a copyright agreement or a T.V. cable subscription). Hyperledger Fabric defines assets with key and value pairs before it is represented (After a state change which will be briefly explained later) as a binary value within the blockchain.

2. Chaincode: The software that applies real-world business logic to the blockchain by organizing creation, modification, and access to the assets within Hyperledger Fabric. The Chaincode is executed with the intention to interact (and mostly update) the current state of the distributed ledger.

3. Ledger and its Features: Ledger is the historical base for all transactions, there are several views for the Ledger (Local and Global, Validated and Peer) which we will discuss in the architecture section. Ledger is composed of a blockchain of blocks which, in turn, consists of several transactions that consist of assets-related activities. Peers are connected to the distributed ledger via channels (which can be private as we explained in the introduction) and each Peer maintains a copy of the ledger for the channel they are members of. The Ledger should support the following functionalities

   a. Modify the Ledger state for any transaction.

b. Retrieve transactions using key lookup queries.

c. Retrieve transactions using range queries.

d. Retrieve transactions using composite queries.

e. Read historical queries.

f. Order transactions into blocks.

g. Deliver transactions to different peers participating on a specific channel.

h. Before committing a block to the blockchain, the ledger must verify that the state was not changed since the Chaincode (which proposed the block) was executed.

i. Channel must support Membership Service Provider (MSP) service to allow different clients to connect to the ledger.

4. Privacy: A ledger exists in a channel, by default any participant should be able to connect to the ledger, however, Hyperledger Fabric can establish private channels where a specific and predefined set of participants only can access the channel and subsequently; the ledger. In such case the participants will use the isolated channel away from the other participants, this can provide support to businesses which need both privacy and decentralization.

5. Membership Service: Hyperledger Fabric provides Membership Service Provider which ensures that trusted participants can join (through their public key). This point

was previously described during the introduction section for Hyperledger Fabric.

6. Consensus: Is the procedure for understanding and agreeing on a specific transaction, Consensus algorithms were discussed during the introductory chapter.

Hyperledger Fabric Architecture

The documentation for Hyperledger Fabric (which is also developed by the open-source community) states four important goals to be achieved by Hyperledger Fabric. The most important thing that we described earlier is **Modularity**. Hyperledger Fabric makes everything as plug & play as much as possible to support more business agility as it is the most important thing in the evolving business nowadays. The implementation effort made to achieve the first goals helps also to achieve the second goal which is **Scalability**, Scalability generally means the ability to scale operations on more computational power. In Hyperledger Fabric The term is used to describe the ability to partition the processing of the chain code between different participating nodes in the network. At the same time, the execution of the chain code is not depending on a single node which will provide more reliability for the whole blockchain.

Another important goal is **Confidentiality** which is achieved through good implementation for both the nodes and the deployment procedure.

And the final goal; **Chaincode trust flexibility** is another important factor where the architecture is separating trust assumptions made for Chaincode from trust assumptions made for ordering transactions, simply, the ordering assumptions and services will be provided from other nodes than those the other nodes which will execute Chaincode.

Transactions

Transactions in Hyperledger Fabric is one of two types, they are:

1. Deploy Transactions: takes the Chaincode program as a parameter and executes it during the deployment of a node.

2. Invoke Transaction: invokes an operation on the previously deployed Chaincode (Through a Deploy transaction). Once the Invoke transaction is successful, it can change the state.
   We can consider the deploy transaction as a subset of invoke transactions as they invoke some operations (though their operations might be not dependent on other operations).

State

State in Hyperledger Fabric is a version of truth for the blockchain. We can talk about state mathematically from the following equation (Pardon me for being a math lover)

$$S = K \rightarrow (V * N)$$

Where S is the state, K is a set of keys within the state, V is a set of values for keys and N is the infinite previous states (or versions) of the blockchain. The structure used here is called the Key / Value Store, which is abbreviated in most cases in the documentation as **KVS**.

Keys in KVS can be related to a specific Chaincode from their name. However, any Chaincode can read keys made by other Chaincodes which is important to support cross Chaincode transactions that are essential for the blockchain to work.

Nodes

Not to be confused, there are three types of nodes under Hyperledger Fabric, they are:

1. Client / Submitting Client: A client that creates, submits and invokes actual transactions. The client acts on behalf of the end-user. And it connects to the peer to be able to communicate with the blockchain (peers and ordering services of other nodes).

2. Peer: A node that commits transactions to the ledger and works (optionally) as an endorser (Remember the Byzantine Generals Problem?). The execution of such activity must occur with respect to the Chaincode. Chaincode will usually contain an endorsement policy that will determine if the Peer if it will allow work as an endorser or not based on some given conditions.

3. Orderer: A node that is responsible for broadcasting orders (also known as ordering service node) is communication implementation that ensures delivery to other nodes participating in the distributed ledger. An Orderer will provide a communication channel to clients and peers to achieve this goal. This channel will allow clients and peers to broadcast messages about their transactions (and other activities like a new node joining the blockchain). The Implementation guarantees that the same message sent from a node will be delivered to all other nodes in the blockchain in the same order (which is essential for the blockchain reliability).
Orderer also supports multiple channels of communication, but when a client connects to a channel (through Orderer) we can totally ignore other channels from programming point of view, however through some

implementations of Hyperledger Fabric we can change the client so it can connect to multiple channels at the same time which is not common in most cases.

Peers and clients connect to the communication channel made by Ordering Service through an API (Ordering Service API) which provides two basic asynchronous events:

a. broadcast(bloc): is called when the client is willing to broadcast a message to the channel (which will be later distributed to the whole blockchain).

b. deliver(seqno, prevhash, blob): is called by the ordering service, not the client. This function delivers the previously broadcasted message to other nodes. seqno is a non-negative integer number represents the sequence number, prevhash is the hash for the most recently delivered blob, and blob is the new message that will be delivered.

A single machine will usually be running on the same physical machine, not to be confused as the division we are using are only from logical perspective but all of them usually run on the same machine (unless some customization effort was made to separate them, which is unlikely as to happen as this will cancel most of the benefits of the blockchain technology usage).

Important properties for the ordering service

The ordering service must apply some properties to ensure blockchain integrity, these properties are:

1. Consistent Agreement: For any two connected peers P1, P2. If P1 is delivering seqno1, prevhash1 and blob1 and P2 receive seqno2, prevhash2 and blob2 then the following conditions must be met

    a. seqno1 and seqno2 are the same.

    b. prevhash1 = prevhash2

    c. blob1 = blob2

2. Hashchain Integrity: for any two events E1 and E2 occurs at a connected peer P1, then
   ```
   deliver(seqno1, prevhash1, blob1) And
   deliver(seqno1+1, prevhash2, blob2)
   ```
   Must satisfy that
   ```
   prevhash = HASH(seqno || prevhash1 ||
   blob1)
   ```

3. No Skipping: Any message was outputted (i.e. the Orderer requested its delivery through delivery(...) event) must have delivered the previous event with the previous sequence number (seqno), previous hash and previous blob message, more specifically
   ```
   deliver(seqno1, prevhash1, blob1)
   ```
   must be called before starting to deliver
   ```
   deliver(seqno1+1, prevhash2, blob2)
   ```

4. No (Direct) Creation: Any call to the event deliver() must be preceded by a call to the event broadcast() at the peer (Actually, it is possible that a call to the event broadcast() occur at peer P1 while the call to the event deliver() be called at peer P2).

5. No Duplication: For any two events E1 and E2 where E1 is a call to
   ```
   broadcast(blob1)
   ```
   And E2 is a call to
   ```
   broadcast(blob2)
   ```
   and other two events E3 and E4 where E3 is a call to

```
deliver(seqno1, prevhash1, blob1)
```
And E4 is a call to
```
deliver(seqno2, prevhash2, blob2)
```
Then the following condition must be met
```
if blob1 == blob2 then prevhash1 ==
prevhash2 and seqno1 == seqno2
```
In other words, if two events are broadcasting and the same blob, then there should be one delivery event that will deliver the same blob with no repetition.
Note: This constraint is not enforced, however, it is strongly recommended to follow it)

6. Liveness: If a client invokes the event broadcast(blob) then all connected peers should trigger the event deliver(seqno, prevhash, blob) to other connected nodes.
Note: in this case, seqno and prevhash are determined by each broadcasting node.

The following steps are describing the lifecycle of a common transaction, we did not consider any different cases of implementations here.

Client Creation of a transaction

Upon client connection to the network, the client will usually be connected to several other peers. To invoke a transaction client will usually send a "PROPOSE" message to a set of selected peers (usually the peers it has connected to before). We will call these peers as "Endorsing Peers". The message is sent using "chaincodeID" which is an ID for identifying the set of endorsing peers. The PROPOSE message is sent to all peers with the chaincodeID provided. Some of these peers might be offline while others might reject the transaction and decide not to endorse it. The client submitting the transaction should try to match the policies for accepting the transaction.

The PROPOSE message is usually on the following format

```
<PROPOSE,tx,[anchor]>
```

The tx parameter is mandatory, while the anchor is optional. tx will be on the following format:

tx=<clientID,chaincodeID,txPayload,timestamp,clientSig>

Where the parameters are

1. clientId: is the id for the client who submitted the transaction proposal.
2. chaincodeID: is the previously described id of the Chaincode.
3. txPayload: is the payload of the transaction
4. timestamp: is a timestamp (generated based on the client local time)
5. clientSig: is the client's signature for the txPayload.

txPayload content will be different if the transaction is an invoke transaction than if it was a deploy transaction. If it is an invoke transaction, then txPayload will contain

1. operation: is the Chaincode operations to be done and its arguments.
2. metadata: is metadata attributes for the invoke transaction.

if the transaction is a deploy transaction, then txPayload will contain

1. source: the source code for the Chaincode to be executed.
2. metadata: is metadata attributes for the deploy transaction.
3. policies: contains policies for the Chaincode, including endorsement policy for transactions.

On the other side, the optional anchor parameter contains read version dependencies for the transaction as key/version pairs.

When a client C1 creates a new message and delivers it to a node with a PROPOSE message, the message can't hold an anchor message as it is a fresh message sent initially by the creator node. If the client will decide to PROPOSE it to the peer P1, then if P1 accepted the transaction and is willing to endorse it, it will send the same PROPOSE message to other peers but after adding anchor information about the original sender. Further details are in the following lines.

After the transaction is issued by a client and sent to an endorsing peer, the peer will first verify the client's signature before anything else, if the signature is valid the peer will check if there are anchor parameters included within the PROPOSE message. if there any, then the peer will read the version numbers. The next step will be simulating the transaction. the peer will invoke the transaction by invoking the Chaincode which the transaction is referring to and will test that against the state of the ledger that the transactions refer to (the most recent version of the ledger before the new transaction was issued).

After this execution (or simulation if you would like to call it so) the endorsing peer will calculate the dependencies (provided in the anchor parameter) and the state updates which is stored as key/value values. when the transaction's Chaincode reads any of these keys the peer will add it to a read set named "readset" and when the transaction modifies any key (or, any newly added keys) the peer will add it to a write set named "writeset", if the readset is equal to the anchor parameter sent in the PROPOSE message the simulation is considered to be valid, if not anchor parameter was sent this condition is skipped.

In the next step, the peer will forward an internal transaction proposal which is called programmatically "tran-proposal" to another component of the peer's logic which is endorsing logic. endorsing logic will accept the transaction by default and sign the "tran-proposalthat If the default scenario occurs the endorsing logic will send a TRANSACTION-ENDORSED message back to the client which submitted the transaction before. accompanied by the transaction Id the Chaincode Id, the blob message, the readset, and the writeset.

If the endorsing logic found the transaction to be invalid, then it will simply reply to the submitting client with a TRANSACTION-INVALID message.

It is important to notice that the state of the ledger wasn't yet changed so far.

Once the transaction is back to the original submitting client with enough number endorsements collected from other peers (if any). The term enough is defined within the Chaincode endorsement policy. Now that both the client and the peer have completed their heaviest work, the Orderer (or ordering service) will start doing the two previously described events. Firstly, the client will invoke the Orderer through the broadcast() event while passing the endorsed transaction (now called "endorsement" programmatically) as the blob parameter. If for some reason the client node is unable to invoke the Orderer it will try to broadcast another peer of its choice. In such cases we call the other peer to be a "Proxy Peer", Proxy peer can damage the message sent which will result in an invalid transaction, therefore it is very important to choose a trusted proxy peer.

Note: if the transaction was not able to get enough endorsements then the client will have two options; either to abandon the transaction or try again later with it.

Note: Proxy Peer cannot change an invalid transaction to be valid, simply because it will miss the correct versioning & signing for it.

After that, the ordering services will start the deliver() event and other peers connected will apply the transaction to their local states, which will eventually become the global state for the distributed ledger.

More on endorsement policies

The Hyperledger Fabric documentation defines endorsement policy as

"A condition on what endorses a transaction"

Endorsement policies must be defined in the blockchain initially so that it can be referenced by the deploy events which will execute transactions specific Chaincode. The endorsement policies should be direct and non-ambiguous as much as possible to ensure a higher level of security, determinism, and performance (The more it gets complex, the more it gets vulnerable).

endorsement policies will provide some logical expressions that will generate either a true or a false result to determine if it will endorse the transaction or not.

For example, if we have the set S of endorsing peers (P1, P2, P3, P4, P5, P6); then we can have any of the following policies (and anything else your imagination can reach as long we can evaluate it as a true or a false result):

1. All Peers within S (P1, P2, ..., P6) must provide a valid signature for the Transaction Proposal "tran-proposal".

2. Any Peer within S (P1 OR P2 OR ... OR P6) must provide a valid signature for the Transaction Proposal "tran-proposal".

3. Some Peers must agree on the Transaction Proposal "tran-proposal" according to the following logical condition *(P1 AND (P2 OR P3) OR P5)*.

4. We can assign different weights to each endorsing peer, for example, P1 can have a weight of 10, while P2 has weight 8, P3 have weight 13, P4 have weight 21, P5 have weight 3 and P6 have weight 30. The total weights for all peers is 85, we can have an endorsement policy that the total weights of endorsing peers must exceed half plus one (43) which will be a dynamically determined value or we can have a static value instead (for example, 50 votes regardless the number of peers and their weights).

The previous conditions are useful in different cases for different applications running for different business flow, the most important thing here is that all of them (and additionally any other logical expressions) are either implemented or easy to implement with Hyperledger Fabric.

The Final Chain: Validated Ledger

Validated Ledger is the final version of the ledger which contains only transactions that were able to satisfy endorsement policies.

The Validated Ledger is sometimes referred to as "VLedger", the first block in the validated ledger is the Genesis block, while the last block (most recent) is the most recently added block of transactions in the blockchain.

Validated Ledger blocks is a subset of the Peer Ledger blocks, Peer Ledger is all blocks for a given peer (including the invalid transactions). However, all invalid transactions are filtered out (through endorsement policy).

Blocks in the validated ledger are chained together in with no errors and in order, each block contains the following:

1. Previous Block Hash (Except for Genesis Block)
2. Validated Block number, programmatically "block".
3. A list of valid transactions committed by peers from the first transaction to the most recent one.
4. The hash of the same block in the peer ledger which is correspondent to the same valid block.

Image source: https://github.com/hyperledger/fabric

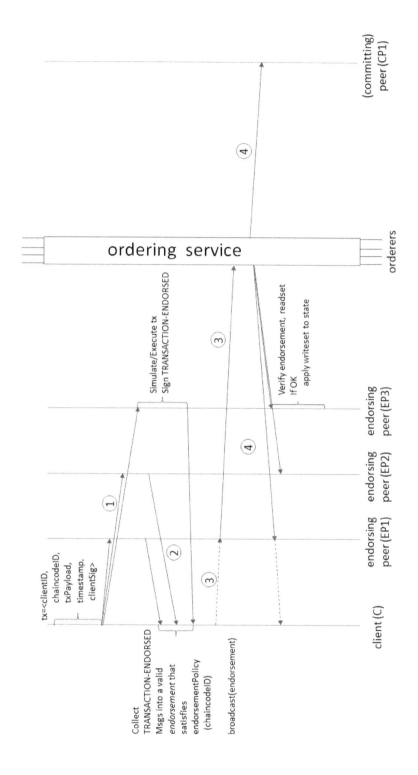

There is a mechanism for filtering out all transactions from the peer ledger into a validated ledger which is called **Checkpointing**; Checkpointing is essential when a new peer is joining the network and is willing to sync with other peers to establish the same version of truth everyone else has. As you might have guessed, the chains for both validated ledger and peer ledger are physically the same on any peer but are separated logically through Checkpointing, in case of some new peers entering the network they don't have to validate the whole chain themselves again and they shall receive the most recent version of the validated ledger from the peers they are connected to.

Peers apply the checkpointing protocol every time new CHK blocks are available where CHK is a configurable parameter for a given number of ledger block. to start checkpointing the peers will broadcast the following message to other connected peers

```
<CHECKPOINT,blocknohash,blockno,stateHash,peer
Sig>
```

where

1. blockno is the current block number
2. blocknohash is the hash for the current block in which its number was provided.
3. stateHash is the hash of the latest state (Produced by Merkle hashes internally, see Merkle hash section under Hyperledger Sawtooth chapter).
4. peerSig is the signature of the current sender peer.

The messages sent will be validated by other peers. The process is similar to the endorsement policies process. The peer collects CHECKPOINT messages from several other peers where

1. blockno of the original message = the blockno for any response message received.
2. the blocknohash is the proper blocknohash for the same block sent.
3. the peerSig is the peerSig for the block received.

It is important to point that checkpoints can be either Local (on the peer level) or Global (on the distributed ledger level). On Global checkpointing, there must be a value (either dynamic or static) for the determination of enough peers to validate a block.

Hyperledger Fabric Certificate Authority Service

Hyperledger Fabric Certificate Authority is an *optional* service that we can use to generate certificates and key materials for managing and configuring identities within the blockchain network.

Hyperledger Fabric Certificate Authority Service (which we will refer to as Authority Service in later lines) uses the Elliptic Curve Digital Signature Algorithm (abbreviated ECDSA) which is the same cryptographic algorithm used by Bitcoin to ensure that Bitcoins can be spent only by its true owners (i.e. You can not use Bitcoins mined by someone else until they transfer them to your own wallet). ECDSA consists of three basic elements and two basic steps, elements are

1. Private Key
2. Public Key
3. Signature

Like other Public and Private Key algorithms, with a different that as any other elliptic curve crypto algorithm; the size of the public key is twice as security level needed and that any two communicating parties should agree on initial elliptic curve field, curve base point, and an integer order or weight of the base point. All these values will work as inputs for the algorithm.

And as you might have already guessed, the two basic operations are signature generation and signature verification.

Note: Any other Certificate Authority Service that uses the ECDSA algorithm can be incorporated inside Hyperledger Fabric.

Hyperledger Fabric Certificate Authority Service runs one Authority Service servers and we can consume it either with Hyperledger Fabric SDKs or via Authority Service Client. In any case, all communications with the Certificate Authority Server must go through REST API. The documentation for the API is available on /swagger directory under GitHub directory for Hyperledger Fabric Certificate Authority Service (And Yes, we are using swagger as we did with Sawtooth).

Further tutorials are available online on Hyperledger Fabric Certificate Authorization Service Repository on GitHub.

Getting Your Machine Ready

Developing a good solution for Hyperledger Fabric involves three main points of view, the first one is the application development which will focus merely on the end-users' application, the second one is network operations and its management while the third point of view is the Chaincode writing itself (Core Development).

Preparing the environment for Hyperledger Fabric is easy. Some basic knowledge of CURL, Docker, Node.js and Go programming language is a big plus if you plan to continue your career as a Hyperledger Fabric Core or Application Developer.

CURL: is a project which provides libraries and command-line interface tools for transferring data between various protocols, it is a nice fact that the name stands for "See URL". CURL library "curlib" is a thread-safe client library that supports cookies, FTP, FTPS, HTTP, HTTPS, IMAP, POP3, SMTP, and RTSP. the library is available for the most used operating systems including (but not limited to) Android, Linux, Windows, macOS, iOS, FreeBSD, OS/2, Solaris and NetBSD.

CURL library "libcurl" also supports IPV6 and we can bind it to 40 different programming languages until the time of writing this book.

To build a good development environment we need to pay some attention to different environments (mainly windows),

Below is a list of tools that we should install to get the environment ready for Hyperledger Fabric:

1. The latest version of CURL.

2. The latest version of Docker. If you're using macOS, Linux or Windows 10 then any version from 17.03.0-ce and higher would do the work, if you're using previous versions of Windows (7/8.1) then you should download Docker Toolbox.

3. The latest version of Go Programming Language, Go is a great programming language by Google, and Chaincode written for Hyperledger Fabric is written in Go too. In Addition, we should make sure that source code (which we will write) is located within the GOPATH environment variable tree. Make sure to add the GOPATH environment variable correctly to your system.

4. Node.js version 6.9 (version 7 is not supported at the time of writing this book).

5. NPM version 3.10 or higher.

Notes for Windows:

1. Before running any "git clone" commands, make sure to run the following commands
```
git config --global core.autocrlf false

git config --global core.longpaths true
```

Because Windows and Linux handle both carriage returns and long file paths in different ways, the first command will cancel automatic handling of carriage return, while the second one will allow long file paths processing so that we will not get "Filename is too long for git for windows ... " errors.

2. Git for Windows and Docker will provide CURL command support automatically once installed but the version included of CURL might be outdated. Please check the CURL version before proceeding, if in doubt, downloading the latest version won't take few seconds!

3. Download Visual Studio C++ Build Tools, this is essential for Node.js to work. Visual Studio C++ Build Tools are available for free download.

4. After installing Visual Studio C++ Build Tools, Install the NPM GRPC module too.

Now your machine is ready with needed tools, execute the following command on the directory where you wish to clone platform binaries

```
curl -SSL https://goo.gl/byy2Qj | bash -s 1.0.5
```

The script will download the four main binaries into /bin folder then it will proceed to download the Docker Image for Hyperledger Fabric into your local Docker registry. There will be two images downloaded, the first one is tagged with "latest" while the second one is tagged with an architecture-specific name (i.e. "x86_64-1.0.1").

SDKs for Hyperledger Fabric are available in both Node.js and Java, Python and Go SDKs will be officially released in the future. Getting SDKs for Java is available through maven, to use the Java SDK in your application add the below code in your pom.xml file

```
<dependencies>
   <dependency>
      <groupId>org.hyperledger.fabric-sdk-java</groupId>
      <artifactId>fabric-sdk-java</artifactId>
      <version>1.0.1</version>
   </dependency>
</dependencies>
```

If you're going to consume SDKs for Node.js, then execute the following command in the desired directory

```
git clone
https://github.com/hyperledger/fabric-sdk-
node.git
```

Understanding YAML

In the next steps, we can expect the reader to be a bit familiar with YAML language, however, this is not extremely needed as YAML language is human-readable. YAML is a data serialization language, configuration files within Hyperledger Fabric are written in YAML, YAML was initially released in 2001 and it became very popular for configuration files and also for other usages when data should be saved in a serializable format.

YAML is Perl Programming language-based, it supports custom data types, but it has been known as a standard to use scalar data types instead, along with lists (also known as arrays) and associative arrays (also known as directories or hashes). Styling in YAML is similar to Python, below are some syntax condition that must be met when writing or editing YAML files:

1. White space indentation is used to make structures while tabs are never allowed as a sign for indentation.

2. To make a comment, type a '#' sign and start typing your comment.

3. Make sure that your '#' sign for comments is preceded by a white space separator from other tokens.

4. List members should be written as one element per line or within curly brackets "{}" or within square brackets "[]".

5. List members should be preceded by a dash '-' sign if they are written in the same

6. Members of a variable must have an indentation in a line following their parent.

7. definition of a container (a list or an associative array) must be preceded by a colon ':' for the container name.

8. Keys and values of an associative array should be separated with a colon sign ':'.

9. multiple lines should be preceded with a '|' sign.

10. multiple lines can also be preceded with a '<' sign.

Many Programming languages support YAML nowadays, this can even lead to making a nice application with an easy to use interface to create different configurations for Hyperledger Fabric environments (Maybe this will become the next tool under Hyperledger Framework umbrella, who knows?)

Examples of YAML syntax follow.

```
# This is a blank comment

key: value # This is a Key / Value Pair

keyNumber1: Value Number One 1 # do you think that keys can have spaces?

integer_key: 120

math_notation: 1e+5

boolean_key: true

otherbooleankey: false

# Setting a key to 1 sets an integer, use true and false for Booleans.

nullkey: null # YAMS support null values.

key with spaces: your question was just answered.

other way to express strings key: "this is a string"

# Yes, both ways are supported to declare a string

"Keys can be quoted too.": "Useful if you want to put a ':' in your key."

this_is_a_multiple_line_string: |
    You should keep the indentation of the string as it is to prevent the
    interpreter from misunderstanding you.

    The String continues until the leading indentation is removed.

folded_style: >
    This one is the same as the above with one exception, the new lines will
    be converted to a white space (per each line).

    The above blank line is expressed as a white space.


# Associative arrays
array_one:
    key1: value1
    key2: value2
    nested associative array:
        keya: keyb
    12.4: 15.1 # keys can be non-string values inside maps.

# lists (or sequences)
countries:
    - United States
    - France
    - Brazil
    - Turkey
    - Germany: Known for good cars production # key and value inside a list
    - United Kingdom
```

Many programming languages provide ready to use support for YAML through ready to use implemented libraries. Search the programming language you are willing to use the documentation for more details and samples.

Building Your First Network Tutorial

The following tutorial is based on the tutorial Provided on the official documentation for Hyperledger Fabric which was prepared with exceeding-expectation attention to details. Cheers to the Open Source Community Contributors!

Make Sure You have empowered your machine with the proper tools as in the previous section, then within your command-line interface; run the following command

git clone https://github.com/hyperledger/fabric-samples.git

This will clone a copy of the Hyperledger Fabric Development Samples to your current directory, there are several tutorials which are:

1. Building Your First Network
2. Writing Your First Application
3. Reconfiguring the Network Built-in Tutorial 1
4. Chaincode for Developers
5. Chaincode for Operators

After you have cloned the Hyperledger Fabric samples repository, navigate with your command line to the */first-network* directory. stay in this directory, for now, if you tried to access the scripts within the /first-network directory outside of the directory itself, the scripts will probably fail to consume binaries which will fail the whole execution.

There is a script file that is "`byfn.sh`", This script file contains commands to initiate the environment, in your command line (Make sure you're still on the same directory), If you run the file with no parameters passed at all, your script will welcome you with the following message:

Usage:

    byfn.sh -m up|down|restart|generate [-c <channel name>] [-t <timeout>] [-d <delay>] [-f <docker-compose-file>] [-s <dbtype>]

    byfn.sh -h|--help (print this message)

      -m <mode> - one of 'up', 'down', 'restart' or 'generate'

        - 'up' - bring up the network with docker-compose up

        - 'down' - clear the network with docker-compose down

        - 'restart' - restart the network

        - 'generate' - generate required certificates and genesis block

        -c <channel name> - channel name to use (defaults to \"mychannel\")

        -t <timeout> - CLI timeout duration in microseconds (defaults to 10000)

        -d <delay> - delay duration in seconds (defaults to 3)

        -f <docker-compose-file> - specify which docker-compose file use (defaults to docker-compose-cli.yaml)

        -s <dbtype> - the database backend to use: goleveldb (default) or couchdb

    Typically, one would first generate the required certificates and genesis block, then bring up the network. e.g.:

    byfn.sh -m generate -c mychannel

    byfn.sh -m up -c mychannel -s couchdb

    byfn.sh -m down -c mychannel

    Taking all defaults:

    byfn.sh -m generate

    byfn.sh -m up

    byfn.sh -m down

An average developer will probably be able to deduce what can this file do (initially) from this message.

The script will initiate the docker image downloaded before (in the previous section) and will initially create a channel with four connected peers representing two different organizations, and an Orderer (Ordering Service) Node.

Initially, the channel names are set to "mychannel", you can change it by passing your favorite channel name as a parameter, however, we will continue working with the default channel name for this tutorial.

write the following command to start execution of the script (with the default variables)

```
./byfn.sh -m generate
```

A confirmation message will show to confirm the generation of the network, type the character 'y' and hit enter.

The script will display a detailed description of all activities it executes, you will notice some interesting things

1. The Genesis block is being generated for the Orderer.
2. Membership Service Provider (MSP) is being created & configured.
3. The Script is creating & configuring the new channel.
4. The Script is creating two Membership Service Providers for each organization.
5. Cryptographic generation "cryptogen" is running.

Once the execution is over, it is time to start the generated network!

In your command line, again, type the following command

write the following command to start execution of the script:

```
./byfn.sh -m up
```

This command will turn on the engine for the generated network, again, the script will display a confirmation message, type the character 'y' and hit enter to proceed.

The script will print the following message on the screen:

```
Starting with channel 'mychannel'
Continue (y/n)?y
proceeding ...
Creating network "net_byfn" with the default driver
Creating peer0.org1.example.com
Creating peer1.org1.example.com
Creating peer0.org2.example.com
Creating orderer.example.com
Creating peer1.org2.example.com
Creating cli
```

```
Channel name: mychannel
Creating channel...
```

As we see, the script has created two peers for each organization (four peers in total) and a single Orderer service after creating the network, then it will proceed to create the communication channel itself. The script will continue execution and the displayed log will grow, take a break for a minute until you see a big END message. this means that everything is ready to use.

Now, let's bring down the network to start inspecting its elements. In your command line, execute the following command:

./byfn.sh -m down

Other confirmation messages will be displayed, type the character 'y' and hit enter to confirm. This command will take down the network created and will delete the created peers and removes the blockchain data from the docker container.

Now Let's inspect some files that control the script behavior. In the /first-network directory we can find several YAML files, these files contain the configuration for different activities which byfn.sh script executes, below are some important points for two of these files:

1. "crypto-config.YAML" file contains definitions for the cryptographic service for nodes. The file contains information about the network topology and allows us (the environment operators) to generate the needed certificates and keys for connected nodes. Every connected organization gets a unique root certificate which keeps the organization's specific components such as peers and ordering services assigned to this organization. This allows all nodes connecting on behalf of an organization to inherit the certificate authority from their organization. It is important to mention that the private key is named "keystore" while the public key is named "signcert". there is also a "count" variable which we use to set the number of peers per organization. There is a standard naming convention for any network entity (which is included in the same file) on the format of HOSTNAME.DOMAIN. for example: organizationX.example.com.

2. "configtx.yaml" file which contains definitions for the network (and channel) configuration, in the previous case there was three main members, one ordering service and two organizations with two peer nodes assigned to each organization. Under the "profile" section within the file, we can see configuration headers for the Genesis block "TwoOrgOrdererGenesis" and for the channel

"TwoOrgsChannel". The "configtx.yaml" file is consumed by the configuration tool "configtxgen". We will use these headers later in the tutorial as arguments for creating artifacts.

3. "docker-compose-cli.yaml" file which contains orderers and peers network information plus several CLI environment settings such as stdin openness, environment paths, and working directories.

Crypto Generator

Hyperledger Fabric comes with the "cryptogen" tool that we can use to generate x509 public key certificates and signatures to use for the cryptographic exchange between network entities.

The Cryptogen tool uses the information within "crypto-config.yaml" file to load network topology. Each organization within the network gets a unique root certificate (ca-cert) provisioned which binds the organization members (orderers and peers) to this specific organization.

Transactions within Hyperledger Fabric Network is signed by the private key of the entity involved in this transaction (code name: keystore) and can be verified (by other entities) using the original entity's public key (code name: signcerts).

Executing "cryptogen" command on the command line interface will result in all certificates and keys generated to be saved into the "crypto-config" folder.

Configuration Transaction Generator

Another tool, the configuration transaction generator (file name: configtxgen) is here to build four configuration (and building blocks) things in the blockchain, they are:

1- The Orderer's genesis block.
2- The Channel's configuration transaction
3- Two transactions for two peers involved in the transaction of the genesis block.

for each one of the above configuration components, a separate command is executed in configtxgen. This is not something that everyday users of your blockchain solutions will do (Genesis Block is the #1 block in any blockchain where other blocks use its [the genesis block] transaction hash to calculate the next transaction hash, and so on). Therefore, you will only need to execute these commands just one time before deploying your blockchain solution into production.

Configtxgen consumes the "configtx.yaml" file which we have described earlier that contains network entities definitions.

Getting Tools to Work

Now Let's run both tools cryptogen and configtxgen to prepare the network to make the next more realistic network startup.

Within your command-line interface, navigate to the /bin directory (if you were not already there) and execute the following command:

```
../bin/cryptogen generate --config=./crypto-config.yaml
```

This command will trigger the crypto generator tool with a "generate" command and sets the crypto-config.yaml as the configuration file.

You will see on your terminal the following output:

```
org1.example.com
org2.example.com
```

This means that certificates and keys have been generated for these two organizations.

If you navigated to your "first-project" root directory. you will see a new folder called "crypto-config" where you can see the certificates and keys generated (which will be the main resource that Membership Service Provider will consume).

Now we need to configure the path for the "configtx.yaml" file. this can be set by the command

```
export FABRIC_CFG_PATH=$PWD
```

The next step will be to execute the configtxgen tool to do the first baby step, genesis block creation!

again (from your bin directory) execute the following command:

```
../bin/configtxgen                    -profile
TwoOrgsOrdererGenesis  -outputBlock  ./channel-
artifacts/genesis.block
```

The command instructs the configtxgen tool to execute based on the TwoOrgsOrdererGenesis profile which we have pointed to previously in the configtx.yaml file, and output the genesis block to the "channel-artifacts" folder which the tool will generate.

An example of the expected output from the command line interface:

```
2018-09-20 12:01:16.104 EDT
[common/tools/configtxgen] main -> INFO 001
Loading configuration
```

```
2018-09-20 12:01:16.108 EDT
[common/tools/configtxgen] doOutputBlock ->
INFO 002 Generating genesis block
```

```
2018-09-20 12:01:16.112 EDT
[common/tools/configtxgen] doOutputBlock ->
INFO 003 Writing genesis block
```

Now we must create the channel configuration transaction (After the successful generation of the genesis block). Before we do that, firstly we need to create a channel configuration transaction to get a channel into the network. Choose a name for your channel and write it down (we will need it in the next few steps). the name should be exactly as a normal variable name.

Now we need to set the selected channel name into our Hyperledger Fabric test network. use the following export command to do so (make sure to replace $CHANNEL_NAME) with your own channel name.

```
export CHANNEL_NAME=mychannel &&
../bin/configtxgen -profile TwoOrgsChannel -
outputCreateChannelTx ./channel-
artifacts/channel.tx -channelID $CHANNEL_NAME
```

Hint: You can save the channel name in an environment variable and use it in your command line instead of remembering it every time.

Example of expected terminal output:

```
2018-09-20 14:14:55.124 EDT
[common/tools/configtxgen] main -> INFO 001
Loading configuration
```

```
2018-09-20 14:14:55.129 EDT
[common/tools/configtxgen]
doOutputChannelCreateTx -> INFO 002 Generating
new channel configtx
```

```
2018-09-20 14:14:55.129 EDT
[common/tools/configtxgen]
doOutputChannelCreateTx -> INFO 003 Writing
new channel tx
```

Now we need to define peers on the two organization (Org1 and Org2). Execute the following commands (And Again, remember to replace the $CHANNEL_NAME with your channel name).

```
../bin/configtxgen -profile TwoOrgsChannel -
outputAnchorPeersUpdate ./channel-
artifacts/Org1MSPanchors.tx -channelID
$CHANNEL_NAME -asOrg Org1MSP
```

```
../bin/configtxgen -profile TwoOrgsChannel -
outputAnchorPeersUpdate ./channel-
artifacts/Org2MSPanchors.tx -channelID
$CHANNEL_NAME -asOrg Org2MSP
```

Starting the Network

Open two terminals, one for executing the CLI calls and the other one is for starting docker compose (to get the network online).

Execute the following command in one of the two terminals, then switch to the other one!

```
docker-compose -f docker-compose-cli.yaml up -
d
```

Note: -d parameter is for detailed log output. if provided, it will show a detailed log (which can be helpful if anything went wrong) but it is still an optional parameter.

Now we need to create and join the channel we have already defined its configuration in the previous step (with configtxgen tool).

Enter the Command-line interface for the docker container by executing this command:

```
docker exec -it cli bash
```

You should see the following output in the terminal:

```
root@0d78bb69300d:/opt/gopath/src/github.com/hyperledger/fabric/peer#
```

Note: the command is running on the default peer (peer0.org1.example.com), if you want to use another peer for that, just override the values of peer0 (or organization1) in the following four environment variables (the values for peer0 comes with the CLI Interface)

```
export
CORE_PEER_MSPCONFIGPATH=/opt/gopath/src/github
.com/hyperledger/fabric/peer/crypto/peerOrgani
zations/org1.example.com/users/Admin@org1.exam
ple.com/msp
export
CORE_PEER_ADDRESS=peer0.org1.example.com:7051
export CORE_PEER_LOCALMSPID="Org1MSP"
export
CORE_PEER_TLS_ROOTCERT_FILE=/opt/gopath/src/gi
thub.com/hyperledger/fabric/peer/crypto/peerOr
```

```
ganizations/org1.example.com/peers/peer0.org1.
example.com/tls/ca.crt
```

Now we need to pass the generated channel configuration transaction as a parameter to the orderer. The channel configuration transaction has been previously saved in the "channel.tx" file. Execute the following command:

```
peer channel create -o
orderer.example.com:7050 -c $CHANNEL_NAME -f
./channel-artifacts/channel.tx --tls --cafile
/opt/gopath/src/github.com/hyperledger/fabric/
peer/crypto/ordererOrganizations/example.com/o
rderers/orderer.example.com/msp/tlscacerts/tls
ca.example.com-cert.pem
```

Replace the $CHANNEL_NAME with your channel name. the -o parameter is for creating the orderer, the -c parameter is for the channel name and the -f parameter is for the channel configuration transaction file. Finally, the –cafile parameter is for the local path to the root certificate of the orderer.

The above command will return a genesis block with the name in the format "CHANNEL-NAME.block". we will use this returned value to join the channel. from now we will assume that the channel name is the default "mychannel" name. If you gave the channel a different name in earlier stages, then you should use it.

The Next step is to join peer0 of organization1 to the channel. Execute the following command in your terminal:

```
peer channel join -b mychannel.block
```

If you want to join more peers in the channel, you will need to provide the appropriate four environment variables as specified at the beginning of "Starting the Network, Again" part of this chapter.

For the next steps, we need to join one more peer (which will be peer 0 from organization 2).

To do so, we need firstly to set the current peer in the command line interface to be peer 0 of organization 2, execute the following commands:

```
peer channel update -o
orderer.example.com:7050 -c $CHANNEL_NAME -f
./channel-artifacts/Org2MSPanchors.tx --tls --
cafile
/opt/gopath/src/github.com/hyperledger/fabric/
peer/crypto/ordererOrganizations/example.com/o
rderers/orderer.example.com/msp/tlscacerts/tls
ca.example.com-cert.pem
```

Then we will add network definition for this peer too (we are adding more data above the genesis block), execute the command:

```
peer channel update -o
orderer.example.com:7050 -c $CHANNEL_NAME -f
./channel-artifacts/Org1MSPanchors.tx --tls --
cafile
/opt/gopath/src/github.com/hyperledger/fabric/
peer/crypto/ordererOrganizations/example.com/o
rderers/orderer.example.com/msp/tlscacerts/tls
ca.example.com-cert.pem
```

Now update the network definitions with appropriate environment variables for peer0.org1

```
CORE_PEER_MSPCONFIGPATH=/opt/gopath/src/github
.com/hyperledger/fabric/peer/crypto/peerOrgani
zations/org2.example.com/users/Admin@org2.exam
ple.com/msp
CORE_PEER_ADDRESS=peer0.org2.example.com:7051
CORE_PEER_LOCALMSPID="Org2MSP"

CORE_PEER_TLS_ROOTCERT_FILE=/opt/gopath/src/gi
thub.com/hyperledger/fabric/peer/crypto/peerOr
ganizations/org2.example.com/peers/peer0.org2.
example.com/tls/ca.crt
```

Getting Started with Chaincode

Chaincode is written in a programming language that handles business logic in a blockchain distributed ledger to make queries or update the ledger state.

This Tutorial is more focused on getting the network itself running. The official documentation for Hyperledger Project provides more tutorials for developing customized Chaincode for Hyperledger Fabric. We will be using an already existing Chaincode here.

There are two available sets of Chaincode available to test, one is written in Golang while the other is written in Node.js. Peers are not dependant on a specific language, meaning that one peer can run Chaincode in Golang while the other can run Node.js Chaincode. We can think of this to integrate different web, mobile or desktop apps into which are using the same ledger in an easier way with no need to implement additional APIs or workarounds.

For installing Golang Chaincode:

```
peer chaincode install -n mycc -v 1.0 -p
github.com/chaincode/chaincode_example02/go/
```

For installing Node.js Chaincode:

```
peer chaincode install -n mycc -v 1.0 -l node
-p
/opt/gopath/src/github.com/chaincode/chaincode
_example02/node/
```

The command will download and install the selected Chaincode from the given GitHub repository (which was already downloaded with samples.)

Now we need to instantiate the Chaincode, instantiation requires specifying the endorsement policy for the Chaincode. As in earlier chapters when we described the Byzantine Generals Problem, there must be a standard policy that we will use to confirm a specific transaction (The Endorsement Policy).

Endorsement Policy has a little syntax to learn, we use it to tell the ledger which condition must be met to confirm a specific transaction. The Endorsement Policy is expressed in a "Principal" format, which comes on the format "MSP.ROLE".

Endorsement Policy Syntax

Endorsement Policy, in general, follows the expression

(EXPRESSION (EXPRESSION(ENTITY, ...) ...)

Where expression is one of three possible expression, and they are:

1- OR
2- AND
3- out of

and role is one of four possible roles, and they are:

1- admin
2- member
3- client
4- peer

Examples:

1- "AND('Org1.member', 'Org2.member', 'Org3.member')"
requests that for each transaction; it must be signed from at least one member of each of the three organizations.

2- "OR('Org1.client', 'Org2.client')"
requests that for each transaction; it must be signed from one client of either organization Org1 or organization Org2.

3- "out of(1, 'Org1.client, 'Org2.client)" is equivalent to the previous OR policy, but we can change the first parameter to be any number of clients needed. (It's not logical to request a single confirmation).

4- "AND(OR('Org1.member','Org2.member'), 'Org3.member')"
requests a signature from Organization Org3 member, AND another signature either from an Org1 member or Org2 member.

Now back on instantiate the Chaincode, we will specify our policy as "AND ('Org1MSP.peer','Org2MSP.peer')". so that we enforce signatures from both Org1 and Org2 peers.

For Golang, Execute

```
peer chaincode instantiate -o
orderer.example.com:7050 —tls —cafile
```

```
/opt/gopath/src/github.com/hyperledger/fabric/
peer/crypto/ordererOrganizations/example.com/o
rderers/orderer.example.com/msp/tlscacerts/tls
ca.example.com-cert.pem -C $CHANNEL_NAME -n
mycc -v 1.0 -c '{"Args":["init","a", "100",
"b","200"]}' -P "AND
('Org1MSP.peer','Org2MSP.peer')"
```

for Node.js, Execute

```
peer chaincode instantiate -o
orderer.example.com:7050 --tls --cafile
/opt/gopath/src/github.com/hyperledger/fabric/
peer/crypto/ordererOrganizations/example.com/o
rderers/orderer.example.com/msp/tlscacerts/tls
ca.example.com-cert.pem -C $CHANNEL_NAME -n
mycc -l node -v 1.0 -c '{"Args":["init","a",
"100", "b","200"]}' -P "AND
('Org1MSP.peer','Org2MSP.peer')"
```

And always remember to replace $CHANNEL_NAME with your previously selected channel name.

Chaincode in Action

Chaincode instantiation can take some time (and Node.js will take more time than Golang). once the instantiation is done, we can start querying the ledge

The previous instantiation commands did an initialization for two values, a and b. the value of a is 100 and the value of b is 200. we will use this information to test our Chaincode in the next step.

Now let's query the ledger for the value of a, execute this command in your command line:

```
peer chaincode query -C $CHANNEL_NAME -n mycc
-c '{"Args":["query","a"]}'
```

You will get the following output:

```
Query Result: 90
```

Now let's make a little change to the ledger by moving the value of '10' from a to b by executing the following invoke-command:

```
peer chaincode invoke -o
orderer.example.com:7050 --tls true --cafile
/opt/gopath/src/github.com/hyperledger/fabric/
peer/crypto/ordererOrganizations/example.com/o
rderers/orderer.example.com/msp/tlscacerts/tls
ca.example.com-cert.pem -C $CHANNEL_NAME -n
mycc --peerAddresses
peer0.org1.example.com:7051 --tlsRootCertFiles
/opt/gopath/src/github.com/hyperledger/fabric/
peer/crypto/peerOrganizations/org1.example.com
/peers/peer0.org1.example.com/tls/ca.crt --
peerAddresses peer0.org2.example.com:7051 --
tlsRootCertFiles
/opt/gopath/src/github.com/hyperledger/fabric/
peer/crypto/peerOrganizations/org2.example.com
/peers/peer0.org2.example.com/tls/ca.crt -c
'{"Args":["invoke","a","b","10"]}'
```

Now we need to check if the previous transaction was completed successfully, let us query the ledger again for the value of a:

```
peer chaincode query -C $CHANNEL_NAME -n mycc
-c '{"Args":["query","a"]}'
```

If everything went fine, we should see the output:

```
Query Result: 90
```

To see the transactions in a detailed log, execute the following command in the command-line interface for your docker container:

```
docker logs -f cli
```

You should see an output like the following (with different hashes indeed):

```
2018-10-01 15:32:18.216 UTC [msp] GetLocalMSP -> DEBU 004 Returning existing local MSP

2018-10-01 15:32:18.216 UTC [msp] GetDefaultSigningIdentity -> DEBU 005 Obtaining
default signing identity

2018-10-01 15:32:18.216 UTC [msp/identity] Sign -> DEBU 006 Sign: plaintext:
0AB1070A6708031A0C08F1E3ECC80510...6D7963631A0A0A0571756572790A0161

2018-10-01 15:32:18.217 UTC [msp/identity] Sign -> DEBU 007 Sign: digest:
E61DB37F4E8B0D32C9FE10E3936BA9B8CD278FAA1F3320B08712164248285C54

Query Result: 90

2018-10-01 15:32:31.351 UTC [main] main -> INFO 008 Exiting.....

====================== Query successful on peer1.org2 on channel 'mychannel'
======================


===================== All GOOD, BYFN execution completed =======================
```

The code behind Chaincode Magic

1- The "script.sh" file, which is in the command-line interface for the container, runs the createChannel command and creates the channel requested using the channel.tx file for channel configuration.

2- createChannel command outputs a genesis block, the genesis block (as any other blockchain block) is saved in each peer's file system containing the channel configuration (previously specified in channel.tx file).

3- the joinChannel command takes the already generated genesis block as a parameter and uses information stored inside to join the channel.

4- The Chaincode sample (saved as "Chaincode_example02") is installed on both anchor peers (peer0.org1 and peer0.org2).

5- The Chaincode is instantiated on peer0.org. This will create a container named "dev-peer0.org2.example.com-mycc-1.0" on peer0.org1.

6- the Chaincode instantiation adds the Chaincode to the channel, and initialize key-value pairs with:

   a. 100

   b. 200

7- A query is made to get the value of a, this will start a container on peer0.org1 named "dev-peer0.org1.example.com-mycc-1.0".

8- The invoke query gets executed to move 10 from a to b. This will install the Chaincode on peer1.org2 (and other peers of org2 if any). This is very important thing to understand; that unless a query that changes the ledger state is executed, we won't get Chaincode installed on other peers. The result is another container named "dev-peer1.org2.example.com-mycc-1.0" started in the peer1.org2 file system. This container is to provide the needed transaction as per the previously defined Endorsement Policy.

To see the Chaincode logs, execute the following command (changing peer and org name won't change the results for all signed transactions.

```
$ docker logs dev-peer0.org2.example.com-mycc-
1.0
```

You should see a similar output to this:

```
04:30:45.947 [BCCSP_FACTORY] DEBU : Initialize
BCCSP [SW]

ex02 Init

Aval = 100, Bval = 200
```

And if we invoke the same query but targeting peer0 of org1

```
$ docker logs dev-peer0.org1.example.com-mycc-
1.0

04:31:10.569 [BCCSP_FACTORY] DEBU : Initialize
BCCSP [SW]

ex02 Invoke

Query Response:{"Name":"a","Amount":"100"}

ex02 Invoke

Aval = 90, Bval = 210
```

```
$ docker logs dev-peer1.org2.example.com-mycc-
1.0
04:31:30.420 [BCCSP_FACTORY] DEBU : Initialize
BCCSP [SW]
ex02 Invoke
Query Response:{"Name":"a","Amount":"90"}
```

So far, we have covered the very basics of knowledge a Hyperledger Fabric network operator should know. There is much customization that can be made. We have used a sample Chaincode to demonstrate that our network is up and running, but no real-world business would only need to store a few values in a ledger. The official documentation (You can find links on Github.com/Hyperledger) provides more than enough details on building custom Chaincode using Chaincode API for both Golang and Node.js.

Chapter 5: Hyperledger Cello

I am personally in love with Cloud computing and its concepts, one great cloud computing perk is the "As A Service" Concept. This concept sent computational limitation to the history especially for the enterprise users; Any Person or organization can use computational resource provided by any cloud provided (which in some cases might be the organization itself) to allocate Hardware and Software Resources for (probably) temporarily or (in some cases) long term use.

The Gate between Hyperledger and Cloud

We can divide Cloud Computation "As A Service" models into three main categories, they are:

1. Infrastructure as a Service (abbreviated Iaas): In this model, we are using the lowest level of computational power from the cloud service provider. We mean by "Lowest Level" the basic hardware level which is (in most cases) the storage disks and the network hardware components.

2. Platform as a Service (abbreviated PaaS): In this model, we are using the medium level of computational power from the cloud service provider. We mean by "Medium Level" the Operating Systems and the database servers which lays between the hardware and the application end users are using directly.

3. Software as a Service (abbreviated SaaS): In this model, we are using a higher level of computational power from the cloud service provider. We mean by "Higher Level" anything an end-user can use, basically software systems and applications; such as CRMs and ERPs.

Back to Blockchain, let's assume two scenarios:

1. Company X is starting a new Blockchain-based business, their business is temporarily but requires many resources to run the blockchain as it is full of media data (images and videos). The **cost of buying enough hardware to run a single node is 50,000 USD**. There are five other companies that will be using the same blockchain along with Company X and for sure they will need to use the same amount of computational resources. The whole **business will end in four months** and none of the five companies (company X and its four business partners) will no longer need to use the hardware they bought.

2. Company Y is starting a new Blockchain-based business, there are several users who will also use the blockchain. Users will need to synchronize their blockchain initially and this will involve synchronization of a big amount of data (10 GB).
   Company Y operates in a developing country and it does not have access to a high quality internet connection to provide synchronization for its users. Company Y will need to install new lines that will cost **100,000 USD** to be able to provide synchronization for its users in the first month of operating the blockchain.
   After the first month, analysis done says that the network will be mature enough that users will be able to synchronize blockchain to each other. And then Company Y will no longer need to use its 100,000 USD network Infrastructure investments.

In both scenarios above, there is a need to use a high amount of computation resources for a short period of time.

In the first scenario, Company X needs to allocate extra ready to use (i.e. operating system and blockchain software) computational power. In this model, there is a need to use the second model (Platform as a Service) or (just assuming it was possible to deploy blockchain directly) the third model (Software as a Service).

While in the second scenario, Company Y needs to allocate additional network infrastructure (i.e. Higher bandwidth and lines). In this model, there is a need to use the first model only where company Y needs to allocate network infrastructure (implicitly accompanies by storage disks for data to be shared over the network and maybe a small server with fast I/O to organize data sharing).

There is a need to go to the cloud solution in both scenarios despite the model Company X or Company Y will use.

So far, everything seems to be smooth and easy, but the real problem is deploying the blockchain itself to the cloud, this is not very easy as it might seem if we are not using Hyperledger Cello.

Hyperledger Cello is a toolkit under the Hyperledger Umbrella that allows using blockchain "As A Service" model and quickly deploy and manage blockchains without additional efforts for installing nodes on machines.

In my opinion, Hyperledger Cello is supporting the usage of a new model which is "Blockchain as a Service" (abbreviated BaaS). The term BaaS was known in 2013 and then became known widely in 2016 and 2017 when global awareness of blockchain technology and cloud computing raised.

Thinking of both cloud computing and Hyperledger Technologies, I see a great chance to use the benefits of both technologies together.

Hyperledger Cello Capabilities

Hyperledger Cello is mainly compatible with Hyperledger Fabric; however, we can do a further modification for it to work with any other blockchain.

The following features are available for Cello users and application developers:

1. Create an instance of the blockchain network instance.

2. Start the blockchain network instance.

3. Stop the blockchain network instance.

4. Delete the blockchain network instance.

5. Customization to the blockchain network from size and consensus algorithm used perspectives.

6. Using blockchain instances with on servers directly or with different containers including vSphere, Docker, Swarm and Kubernetes with more support to be available in the future.

7. Using blockchain instances on different architectures including x86, ARM and Z.

8. Several operational activities such as logging, monitoring and health management.

9. Quickly build a blockchain from scratch.

10. Provision instances quickly with no additional effort once they are created.

11. Use of an easy to use Dashboard via a web interface.

Cello Architecture

Using Terminology of Hyperledger Cello, each running instance is a **node** and each set of nodes operating together in a cluster is simply called **cluster** and it includes several peer nodes which might be Hyperledger Fabric, Hyperledger Sawtooth or Hyperledger Iroha chain.

Hyperledger Cello using the Microservices concept. The Microservices concept allows decoupling most of the system features into several small services. Microservices is also a variation of Service Oriented Architecture (abbreviated SOA). I personally consider such a concept to be an extension of the DevOps concept explained in the earlier part of this book.

Another important concept was considered while developing Hyperledger Cello is the scalability and fault-tolerance. Hyperledger Cello can be scaled to whatever needed number of nodes to operate and it will also tolerate if there is a failure because of good implementation of Microservices that constructs it.

Hyperledger Cello operates on three main levels, they are:

1. Access Layer: includes Web UIs to be managed directly by the users.
2. Orchestration Layer: handles requests from the Access Layer and make calls to agents to operate the blockchain resources as requested.

3. Agent Layer: the real workers working under the Master Node.

Each layer maintains a stable API for the upper layers to maintain higher decoupling with no need to change other layers.

Hyperledger Cello follows the Master – Worker architecture, in each cluster, there is typically a single Master Node and several Worker Nodes.

The Master nodes hold cello services and the official documentation recommends running it on a modern version of either Linux or macOS. The Master node manages the worker nodes through the worker node's API. You can access the Master node's dashboard through port 8080 and its REST API through port 80. Each Master Node has three main services, they are:

1. Dashboard: UI Dashboard
2. Rest Server: Server for REST API
3. Watchdog: For Maintaining health checking.

The Worker nodes hold the blockchain, they can be heterogeneous (i.e. one of them can be running on docker, another on vSphere while the other is running directly on a physical server). Worker nodes' API can be accessed through port 2375.

Any pool of resources managed by the same control point (Master) is referred to as **Host** as long as these resources are grouped together. Each resource might be a Docker host, Swarm cluster or a physical server cluster. The host is usually managed by the same resource controller.

Each host usually has the following properties:

1. A **Name** that is human readable.
2. A **Demon URL** for the Docker or Swarm access.

3. A **Capacity** for how many maximum chains the host can have.
4. A **Logging Level** for logging chains in the host.
5. A **Logging Type** to handle log messages.
6. A **Schedulable** data about host availability to be scheduled for users.
7. An **Autofill** option to automatically fill the host with chains.

Each chain has also several properties, they are:

1. A Name that is human readable.
2. A Host where the chain operates.
3. A size for the number of nodes the chain can have.
4. A Consensus which is the type of consensus this chain uses.

To quickly recap the architecture, each Master node manages a set of blockchain networks running in the worker nodes. Each set of worker nodes is grouped under a Host and each of these worker nodes runs one or more chains.

Getting Started with Hyperledger Cello

Setting Your Master Node

To Set a Master Node, we need to have a modern machine (8 Virtual CPUs, 16 GB RAM and 100 GB Diskspace) and several software components, they are:

1. Docker Engine 1.10 or higher (except Docker 17.0 as its support is still experimental).
2. Docker Compose 1.8.0 or higher.
3. Bother Git and Make installed on your machine.

Next, we will need to clone the Hyperledger Cello repository, simply in your terminal run the following commands

```
git clone
http://gerrit.hyperledger.org/r/cello
cd cello
```

The repository cloned contains several folders, most of the time we will use scripts ready to use under the /scripts directory. A local copy of the documentation also exists in the /docs directory. I recommend taking a quick look at the repository once it is cloned.

The Next thing to do would surely be setting up the Master node, just run the following command in your terminal

```
make setup-master
```

this command will consume the setup.sh script under the /scripts directory. Nothing will crash if you repeat this command. It is also a clever idea to check that no errors occurred during the setup, you can check logs after the setup is done with the following command

```
make logs
```

Now to start the whole services, simply execute the following command in your terminal

```
make start
```

to redeploy a specific service (useful if you made any changes to it); execute the following command in your terminal

```
make redeploy service=SERVICE_NAME
```

replace SERVICE_NAME with the name for service you wish to redeploy, example

```
make redeploy service=dashboard
```

you can also apply the service filter while reading logs, for example, if you want only to check logs from the dashboard service, execute

```
make log service=dashboard
```

To access your dashboard, simply in your browser go to the following URL

```
MASTER_IP:8080
```

Replace MASTER_IP with the IP for your master node, example

```
192.168.13.2:8080
```

for access to the API (if you plan to use it directly for some reason) use port 80 instead.

Hint: If you are using macOS, make sure to have the path /opt/cello/mongo created, this path is used for data storage. Also, make sure that the file-sharing is on for this path, so it can be mounted with Docker.

To build a docker image and commit it to your local environment, simply run

```
make docker
```

This above command uses the Hyperledger Cello Base Image, which works as a middle layer between your operating system configuration and the customizations required for Hyperledger Cello.

Here is a list of additional useful commands with make

1. The make all command will run all the test cases.

2. To clean up your environment from the cache and temporary files, run the following two commands
```
$ rm -rf .tox .cache *.egg-info

$ find . -name "*.pyc" -o -name
"__pycache__" -exec rm -rf "{}" \;
```

3. To make a local version of the docs available, run

```
pip install mkdocs
mkdocs serve
```

4. If you are stuck in the middle of something and need help, just type help to access rich help content for all commands.

Setting Up your Worker Node

There are several types of Worker Nodes, in this example We will go for a Docker Host running as a Worker node and will go also for vSphere in another example, additional information for setting up other types of workers can be found on the official documentation

Setting Up Worker Node for Docker Host

Requirements for a Docker Host working as a worker node is the following:

1. A modern machine, with 8 virtual CPUs and 16 GB of RAM and 100 GB of disk space.
2. Docker Engine 1.10.0 to 1.13.0
3. If you are using Ubuntu 14.04, install aufs-tools.

Configure your Docker Deamon to listen to port 2375 and make sure that the port and node are discoverable through your network configuration.

If you are using Ubuntu 16.04 or higher, update your /lib/system/system/docker.service with the following configuration

[Service]

```
DOCKER_OPTS="$DOCKER_OPTS -H
tcp://0.0.0.0:2375 -H
unix:///var/run/docker.sock --api-cors-
header='*' --default-ulimit=nofile=8192:16384
--default-ulimit=nproc=8192:16384"
```

```
EnvironmentFile=-/etc/default/docker
```

```
ExecStart=
```

```
ExecStart=/usr/bin/dockerd -H fd://
$DOCKER_OPTS
```

Then Regenerate your Docker service script, execute the following command

```
systemctl deamon-reload
```

then restart the docker engine, execute the following command

```
systemctl restart docker.service
```

If you are using Ubuntu 14.04, open Docker config file available in /etc/default/docker and add the following line to it

```
DOCKER_OPTS="$DOCKER_OPTS -H
tcp://0.0.0.0:2375 -H
unix:///var/run/docker.sock --api-cors-
header='*' --default-ulimit=nofile=8192:16384
--default-ulimit=nproc=8192:16384"
```

If you are using MacOS, there is no direct way to configure your Docker deamon to listen to the network, use any tool for networking with Mac to do so then configure your Docker deamon to listen to the port 2375 with the following command (assuming connection to 127.0.0.1)

```
$ docker run -d -v
/var/run/docker.sock:/var/run/docker.sock -p
127.0.0.1:2375:2375 bobrik/socat TCP-
LISTEN:2375,fork UNIX-
CONNECT:/var/run/docker.sock
$ docker -H 127.0.0.1:2375 info
```

The Next step is (independent from your operating system) is to execute setup worker command, simply execute the following command in your terminal

make setup-worker

Also make sure that your IPV4 forward is enabled, you can run the following command to be sure

```
$ sysctl -w net.ipv4.ip_forward=1
```

Setting the worker node for vSphere

The list of steps for vSphere is a bit long, I will assume that the reader is a bit familiar with vSphere.

The prerequisites are:

1. Make sure that time is synced in all ESXi Hosts in the cluster that Hyperledger Cello services will use. This is very important as if time is not synced then certificates issued during deployment will be out of date for other ESXi hosts.

2. Make sure to have vSphere vCenter 6.0 or 6.5, the official documentation confirms that only tested versions are those.

3. The Hyperledger Cello vSphere agent works only on vSphere with vCenter, if you have a single vSphere node only without vCenter then your deployment will fail.

4. Make sure to have a DHCP server in the VM network, if your VMs can get an IP automatically then this means you have a DHCP server already within your VM network.

5. Make sure that you have a vCenter user with the following set of privileges:

   a. Allocate space in the Datastore.
   b. Low-Level File Operations in the Datastore.
   c. Create Folders
   d. Delete Folders
   e. Assign a network
   f. Assign a virtual machine to the resource pool
   g. Add a new disk to a virtual machine
   h. Add an existing disk to a virtual machine
   i. Add devices to a virtual machine
   j. Remove devices from a virtual machine
   k. Change CPU count for a virtual machine
   l. Change resources for a virtual machine
   m. Configure Memory for a virtual machine
   n. Change device settings for a virtual machine
   o. Remove disk from a virtual machine
   p. Rename a virtual machine
   q. Change settings for a virtual machine
   r. Change advanced settings for a virtual machine
   s. Power On a virtual machine
   t. Power Off a virtual machine
   u. Create a virtual machine from an existing one (from inventory)
   v. Create a new virtual machine (from inventory)

w. Remove a virtual machine (from inventory)

x. Clone a virtual machine

y. Customize a virtual machine

z. Read customization specifications for a virtual machine

aa. Import-Profile-driven for vApp

bb. view storage for Profile-driven.

After you make sure that this list of permissions is set. The next step will be to upload a VM image to be used on the vSphere. Upload the template OS OVA to vCenter before you create a vSphere type host in Hyperledger Cello. We will clone one or several work nodes runs Hyperledger Fabric (or other blockchains) workloads from this VM Template.

The Next step is to upload the VM with vSphere Client, Login to your vSphere Client, Right Click on the ESX Host which have the permissions listed earlier and select the Deploy OVF Template option.

You will be prompted to enter A URL for the OVA image, use the image from this URL provided by the official documentation:

https://drive.google.com/file/d/0B4Ioua6jjCH9b0ROOE14SUIqU k0/view

Make sure to deploy the OVA to the same cluster you will use for Hyperledger Cello later.

Also, remember the name of the VM you have created as it vSphere will use it to create a vSphere type host in Hyperledger Cello. The default name should be "PhotonOSTemplate.OVA".

The OVA image is based on Photon OS 2.0.

Do not power on the imported virtual machine, to prevent future clones of this VM from using the same IP address, you must execute the following command first

```
echo -n > /etc/machine-id
```

Then you can start your VM.

The next steps will be the same as it will be for Docker Host, except that you will need to add more details for the vSphere when you add a host. Continue with the next part normally and prepare the following information about your VCenter environment:

1. VC IP Address
2. VC Username
3. VC Password (You will need to enter it in plain text, make sure no one is behind :))
4. VC Network Name
5. Datacenter Name
6. Cluster Name
7. Datastore Name

Additional data for your VM settings will be also requested, the details needed are:

1. VM IP
2. VM Gateway
3. VM Netmask
4. VM DNS
5. VM Virtual CPUs count
6. VM Memory in GBs.
7. VM Template Name

All remaining steps will be the same for Docker Host.

Adding Host and Chain

When you start Hyperledger Cello for the first time, you will need to add your host to it, go to your dashboard in your browser by accessing the Master Node URL through port 8080.

You will be prompted to enter credential to access the dashboard, use the default credentials for admin which is

```
Username: admin
```

```
Password: pass
```

To add a host, go to the hosts page and click the Add Host button on the top right corner.

You will be prompted through a dialog to enter the host details, give your host an easy-to-understand name, add the daemon URL for your host followed by port number (2375), so it should something like

```
192.168.1.21:2375
```

Set the maximum capacity of the host, depending on how many chains your host can handle.

Set logging level and logging type to whatever you need. then check the Schedulable checkbox if you need to schedule this host for cluster request.

After you add your host, you can find it in the Host Page, with the capacity provided and zero chains.

The Next step will be to create and add chains to the host, Go to the active chain page which should be empty by default, click the Add Chain button on the top right corner, you will be prompted by a dialog to add chain information, add the chain Name, make sure it is readable and meaningful name, then select a host, chain size and your consensus plugin (representing the consensus technique to be used) and finally, click the create button.

The active chain page will now display the created chain.

More on the Admin Dashboard

If you want to add several chains automatically, you can use the fill-up option, from your host action drop-down menu you can click the Fill up button to full to host with chains as per the host's capacity automatically.

If you want to clean up the unused chains from the host, you can click the clean button from the same drop-down menu.

The homepage for the dashboard is the overview page, the overview page as you might have guessed from its name; shows a high-level overview of the system status.

The Overview page displays a general system overview where you can see the number of working hosts, the number of active chains and the number of released chains.

The page also displays the host status, dividing hosts into active and inactive hosts. And it also displays the chain statues and how many of the currently active chains are utilized by the users.

The dashboard also contains a dedicated page for the system status, where you can access quick information about your Hyperledger Cello system, such as

1. Host Types: either single or swarm hosts.
2. Host status: either active or inactive.
3. Chain Type (or consensus type)
4. Chain status: either free or used.

Another important page is the hosts page, you can see there a table of hosts available, their types, status, number of chains, capacities, log levels, and types and for each host in a row, you can see the drop-down menu for actions.

Additional actions than fill up and clean are:

1. config: you can change the configuration of a host that was previously added.

2. Reset: you can reset everything running on a given host, this is very useful when there is a problem with chains on the host.

3. Delete: you can delete the host from your Hyperledger Cello environment.

The Next Page is the Active chains page which we passed through quickly earlier, the Active chains page contains everything about the chains in your Hyperledger Cello environment, you will see a table for all chains available, displaying its name, consensus type, status, health, size, host and an action drop-down menu. You can do several things with it (the action drop-down menu), these actions are:

1. Start the chain.
2. Stop the chain with its status.
3. Restart the chain
4. Delete the chain.
5. Release the chain (this releases the chain used by a user to the pool again). This option will be disabled if the chain is already started and you will need to stop it first.

Now as both companies; X and Y are happy, you can feel free to try other options available within the dashboard.

The User Dashboard

There is another dashboard for the user, the previously discussed dashboard is the Hyperledger Cello Admin dashboard where operators can do most of the work smoothly. The User dashboard also makes it easier for users to consume chains allocated which we have had discussed in the previous pages.

We can access the user dashboard through port 8081 on the Master Node, you can use the same credentials which is

Username: admin

Password: pass

to access the user dashboard. The user dashboard consists of three main pages for accessing important information about the chain and smart contracts running on the chain.

The first page is the Chain Page, the chain page displays general information about the chain in action, this information is:

1. The number of peers connected to the chain.
2. The number of blocks in the blockchain.
3. The number of smart contracts in action.
4. The number of transactions.
5. The type of the chain (Fabric, Sawtooth or Iroha).
6. The Hours the chain has been running.
7. The Chain's name.

8. The recent blocks in the chain and its transactions, creation time and Id.
9. The recent transactions, its content and creation time.

The second page is the Invoke Page, where you can invoke or query a smart contract API and get a response from it, the page contains just the input fields needed for invoking a smart contract, which is:

1. The smart contact Id.
2. The function's name.
3. The parameters to be sent.
4. The Method (either invoke or query).
5. A submit button.

The third and last page is the smart contract page, on this page, we can do any of the following:

1. Upload a smart contract.
2. Install a smart contract.
3. instantiate a smart contract.
4. delete a smart contract.
5. See and manage existing smart contracts.

API V2

The Web UI for Hyperledger Cello's dashboards communicates with the service itself through a RESTful API, the first version of the API (API V1) was depreciated by Hyperledger Cello contributors and it is strongly recommended to use V2 Instead. We will go for a quick overview of API V2 instead of API V1.

We can access the API via port 80 and all calls to the API should append the /vs prefix, for example:

```
Machine_IP:80/cluster_op
```

```
should be replaced with
```

```
Machine_IP:80/v2/cluster_op
```

```
API supports both POST and GET methods,
example for Cluster Apply using POST
```

```
POST /cluster_op
{
action:xxx,
key:value
}
```

The same call can be achieved with the GET method:

```
GET /cluster_op?action=xxx&key=value
```

The actions supported by API V2 are the following:

1. Release: to release a chain, we can not release a chain if it is running.
2. Apply: to apply a chain.
3. Start: start a chain.
4. Restart: to restart a chain.
5. Stop: to stop a chain.

Any of these calls should be accompanied by a key for the chain to be stopped, released or whatever action to take.

The Cluster Apply call applies a cluster that is available to be allocated for a user. This cluster apply command supports multiple filters, here is an example

```
POST /cluster_op
{
action:apply,
user_id:xxx,
allow_multiple:False,
consensus_plugin:pbft,
consensus_mode:batch,
size:4
}
```

The REST Server will return the following response if the previous request succeeded.

```
{
  "code": 200,
  "data": {
```

```
    "api_url": "http://192.168.7.62:5004",
    "consensus_mode": "batch",
    "consensus_plugin": "pbft",
    "worker_api": "tcp://192.168.7.62:2375",
    "id": "576ba021414b0502864d0306",
    "name": "compute2_4",
    "size": 4,
    "user_id": "xxx"
  },
  "error": "",
  "status": "OK"
}
```

Another example for releasing a specific cluster request
POST /cluster_op
```
{
action:release,
cluster_id:xxxxxxxx
}
```

And if this release request succeeded then the REST API V2
will respond with
```
{
  "code": 200,
  "data": "",
  "error": "",
```

```
  "status": "OK"
}
```

You can also release all cluster under a specific user's account, example

```
POST /cluster_op
{
action:release,
user_id:xxxxxxxx
}
```

Another example for starting a cluster:

```
POST /cluster_op
{
action:start,
cluster_id:xxx,
node_id:vp0
}
```

To List all clusters of a given type and size

```
POST /clusters
{
consensus_plugin:pbft,
consensus_mode:classic,
size:4,
user_id:""
}
```

To query a cluster for a specific user:

```
POST /clusters
{
user_id:xxx
}
```

And Finally, to get an object of a cluster:

```
GET /cluster/xxxxxxx
```

Recommended Configuration for Production Environment

The Hyperledger Cello Official Documentation strongly recommends few settings to be applied to your environment for improved performance, these settings are:

1. Open the file /etc/sysctl.conf and append the following configuration
```
vm.swappiness=10
fs.file-max = 2000000
kernel.threads-max = 2091845
kernel.pty.max = 210000
kernel.keys.root_maxkeys = 20000
kernel.keys.maxkeys = 20000
net.ipv4.ip_local_port_range = 30000 65535
net.ipv4.tcp_tw_reuse = 0
net.ipv4.tcp_tw_recycle = 0
net.ipv4.tcp_max_tw_buckets = 5000
net.ipv4.tcp_fin_timeout = 30
net.ipv4.tcp_max_syn_backlog = 8192
```
2. Run the following command
```
sysctl -p
```
3. Open the file /etc/security/limits.conf and append the following configuration
```
* hard nofile 1048576
* soft nofile 1048576
```

```
* soft nproc 10485760
* hard nproc 10485760
* soft stack 32768
* hard stack 32768
```

Chapter 6: Hyperledger Composer

Hyperledger Composer is a tool to allow fast creation of customized blockchains based on the Hyperledger Fabric Network. The official tutorial contains well-detailed instructions on almost everything related to Hyperledger Composer. You can find it under GitHub Account for Hyperledger Project.

The main difference between Hyperledger Composer and Hyperledger Cello is the level of easy to use customization. Hyperledger Cello focuses on scalability while Hyperledger Composer is more customization oriented. However, it is possible to use Composer to build your customized blockchain and then use Hyperledger Cello to deploy as many instances as you need.

Hyperledger Composer official documentation classifies it as a development framework, however, as it depends on Hyperledger Fabric I preferred to list it as a tool or a module instead for clarity purpose.

Introducing and Recapping Hyperledger Composer

Hyperledger Composer is an open-source toolset and framework to develop blockchain applications faster, the project aims to reduce the effort needed to create and deploy blockchains. I personally feel the spirit of DevOps concept here as Hyperledger Composer makes more automation for the blockchain development lifecycle. One more perk of Hyperledger Composer is the integrability with other existing systems, so it should be a good transitional point for any existing business moving to the blockchain technology.

The mainstream support in Hyperledger Composer is for Hyperledger Fabric blockchain, Hyperledger Fabric was chosen in most tools under the Hyperledger Umbrella as it supports consensus to be used as plug and play.

Hyperledger Composer allows modeling your existing business (or a new one) into an easy to understand structure consists mainly of three elements, these elements are:

1. Assets: An Asset is anything that can be sold or have a value, for example, houses and cryptocurrencies.

2. Participants: A participant is any entity that buys and sells assets on a blockchain.

3. Transactions: An activity involves one or more participants and one or more assets.

You can control the access level given to participants based on your business flow.

Hyperledger Composer Architecture

Hyperledger Composer is quite dynamic when it comes to implementing your own business flow into a reasonable architecture. However, a typical architecture consists of the following high-level components:

1. Execution Runtimes: Hyperledger Composer supports Three execution runtimes until the time of writing this book. These runtimes are:

   a. Hyperledger Fabric 1.0 State saved on a distributed ledger.

   b. Web with state saved in the browser's local storage.

   c. Embedded; executes with Node.JS process and usually used for business application unit testing. where the state is saved in a memory key/value store.

2. JavaScript SDK: Hyperledger Composer JavaScript SDK is a set of APIs built with Node.JS which allows developers to create business useful applications quickly. There are two APIs in two npm modules, these APIs are:

   a. composer-client: used to submit transactions to the business network to create, delete, update and retrieve transactions, assets and participants. We will install this usually on a local dependency of the user application to allow the user to connect to the business network and access transactions, assets, and participants.

    b. composer-admin: used to manage the blockchain network itself. We will install this module as a local dependency for administrative applications responsible for deploying and undeploying the business network. This module also allows the creation of business network definitions.

3. Connection Profiles: We use connection profiles to specify how to connect to the runtimes. different types of execution runtimes are supported when it comes to connectivity options, for example, if we are using Hyperledger Fabric 1.0 then we will use the TCP/IP addresses and ports to connect to peers. connection profile documents are in JSON format.

4. Command Line Interface: allows developers and operators to control and modify business network definitions.

5. REST Server: Hyperledger Composer comes with a ready to use automatically generated Open API (Swagger API) for the business network. The REST server transforms the composer model into an API that follows Open API definition to allow runtimes to create, update, delete and retrieve assets, participants and transactions.

6. Loopback Connector: Loopback Connector is a component consumed by the REST Server or as a standalone module by different integration tools that support loopback. It might be also used to create more advanced versions of the REST APIs.

7. Playground Web User Interface: a web interface used to define, manage and test business networks. The Playground targets business analysts to allow them to quickly prototype business logic to the blockchain (Fabric, Web or whatever interface they will use).

8. Yeoman Code Generators: Yeoman code generator is an open-source framework used to create skeleton projects. Hyperledger Composer uses it to create Node.JS application, Angular Web app, and skeleton business network.

9. Editor Extensions: this is development-related more than architecture-related; Hyperledger Composer has two extensions to use for development of its applications, these extensions are:

   a. Visual Studio Code Extension: Visual Studio Code is a free to use editor by Microsoft, the community has contributed with an extension for developing Hyperledger Composer based applications on Visual Studio Code. This extension is great when it comes to validating Hyperledger Composer Models, validating ACL files, syntax highlighting, error detections and code snippet support.

   b. Atom Editor Plugin: This plugin has only basic syntax highlighting support.

More on Hyperledger Composer Concepts

A few additional concepts related to Hyperledger Composer are important for Blockchain application Developer to understand, we will go quickly for these concepts in the next lines.

Each participant in the business network gets a unique identifier that we call **Identity**. The given identity along with participant metadata and connection profile is combined by Hyperledger Composer into what we know as **Id Card**. Usage of Id Cards makes it easier to connect participants to business networks.

A **Query** is a request for data from the blockchain. Using Hyperledger Composer we can define queries within the business network exactly as we define assets and participants. We can execute queries through Hyperledger Composer API.

Access Control is a set of rules to make sure that every participant can only access data they are authorized to know under their current condition; for example, a homeowner can access private details about the homeowner identity only if the home asset belongs to them. but they can not access the homeowner's identity for other homes as we consider this as private information. The access control is not limited to accessing the data but also to modify it; if we are talking about the same home then no one can sell the home unless they are its owners.

Historian Registry is a registry where all records of successful transactions are stored. We call any transaction in the Historian Registry to be a **Historian Record** which contains details about participants, their identities and assets involved.

Starting Development with Hyperledger Composer

You can use Hyperledger Composer to develop applications either on Linux or macOS. The official documentation recommends at least 4 GB of memory space available.

Ubuntu Installation

We will need the following prerequisites to be installed on your ubuntu machine to proceed:

1. Ubuntu 14.04 to 16.04 64 bit.
2. Docker Engine 17.03 or higher.
3. Docker Compose 1.8 or higher.
4. Node 8.9 or higher (version 9 is not supported).
5. npm v5.x
6. Git 2.9 or higher.
7. Python 2.7.x
8. A code editor (Visual Studio Code is recommended).

The good thing here is that Hyperledger Composer community provides a ready to use package containing all needed components, you only need CURL installed to use it, simply execute the following commands in your terminal:

```
curl -O
https://hyperledger.github.io/composer/prereqs
-ubuntu.sh
```

```
chmod u+x prereqs-ubuntu.sh
```

Then run the prereqs-ubuntu.sh by executing the command:

```
./prereqs-ubuntu.sh
```

The official documentation has several bits of advice for Linux users, they are:

1. Log in as a normal user, not root.
2. Use CURL to install prerequisites, then unzip them using sudo.
3. Run prereqs-ubuntu.sh as a normal user, if prompted for a root password, then enter it.
4. Do not use npm with sudo or su,
5. avoid installing node as root.

macOS Installation

On macOS, we will need to install the following:

1. nvm (Node version manager which is a tool that allows to easily install or uninstall different versions of Node).
2. Apple XCode.

to install nvm, open your terminal and execute the following command

```
curl -o-
https://raw.githubusercontent.com/creationix/n
vm/v0.33.0/install.sh | bash
```

execution of the above command will trigger git commands, you will be prompted to install XCode if you do not have it, click on Get XCode from the dialog if it appears.

After XCode finishes the installation, execute the following command to create your bash profile

```
touch .bash_profile
```

then run the first command again

```
curl -o-
https://raw.githubusercontent.com/creationix/n
vm/v0.33.0/install.sh | bash
```

The next step will be switching your Node environment to the long-term support (stable) release, execute the following command:

```
nvm-use —lts
```

Then, install Docker on Mac by downloading the dmg file that can be found easily on Docker Website.

Finally, we will need to install Visual Studio Code and add Hyperledger Composer extension to it, in your browser navigate to Visual Studio Code website "code.visualstudio.com" and download Visual Studio Code for Mac and install it.

After Visual Studio Code is installed, open it and click on the extensions option from the toolbar, type "Hyperledger Composer" in the search bar to find Hyperledger Composer extension for Visual Studio and install it, once it is installed, restart Visual Studio Code to activate the extension.

Installing the Development Environment

After we have successfully acquired the needed prerequisites, the next step is to install the development environment for Hyperledger Composer itself, we will need to install several components, they are:

1. Essential CLI tools: run the following command in your terminal
   ```
   npm install -g composer-cli
   ```

2. The REST server local instance: run the following command in your terminal
   ```
   npm install -g composer-rest-server
   ```

3. Application Utility Generation tool: run the following command in your terminal
   ```
   npm install -g generator-hyperledger-composer
   ```

4. Yeoman generation tool: run the following command in your terminal
   ```
   npm install -g yo
   ```

The Next step is to install Hyperledger Composer Playground, the playground is the most important and easy to use component of Hyperledger Composer. The Community even recommends the usage of the web version of the online playground for totally inexperienced users (and even non-developers) to the blockchain technology so that they can learn in practice more concepts about the blockchain technology.

You can access the online Playground (web version) from the official website for Hyperledger Composer, using the online playground you can define assets, create participants and execute transactions on behalf of participants. However, we will go for installing a local version of the Hyperledger Composer playground as we are preparing the local machine, so we will not depend on the Web Playground for now (Through I really recommend looking at it before proceeding). The local version is also a web version, but it runs locally on your machine. Simply execute the following command in your terminal:

```
npm install -g composer-playground
```

Now as we are ready with Hyperledger composer components and prerequisites, we need to prepare Hyperledger Fabric Runtime, so we can depend on it as a chain provider.

In your terminal, execute the following commands:

```
mkdir ~/fabric-tools && cd ~/fabric-tools
```

```
curl -O
https://raw.githubusercontent.com/hyperledger/
composer-tools/master/packages/fabric-dev-
servers/fabric-dev-servers.zip
unzip fabric-dev-servers.zip
```

For tar.gz instead, just replace zip with tar.gz.

Now to download the local runtime for Hyperledger Fabric, navigate to the fabric tools directory, execute:

```
cd ~/fabric-tools
```

then execute the fabric downloader script, simply execute:

```
./downloadFabric.sh
```

Once the download is complete, everything will be ready for a normal developer to start work. Other Several activities can be done with your environment to manage it, they are:

1. Starting Hyperledger Fabric runtime, execute the following commands in your terminal:

```
cd ~/fabric-tools
./startFabric.sh
./createPeerAdminCard.sh
```

The last command generated an Id Card for an admin, use it only in the very first time you start Hyperledger Composer.

2. Stopping Hyperledger Fabric runtime, execute the following commands in your terminal:

```
~/fabric-tools/stopFabric.sh
```

If you want to remove Id Card issues for your peer admin, use this command in your terminal:

```
~/fabric-tools/teardownFabric.sh
```

Note: If you are using the teardown script, you will need to generate a new Peer Admin Id Card the next time you start Hyperledger Fabric runtime.

3. To start the local Hyperledger Composer Playground Web App, execute the following command in your terminal:

```
composer-playground
```

A new window will be opened in your default web browser to access your localhost at port 8080 asking for credentials. Use the PeerAdmin@hlfv1 Card that was created by the create peer admin card script which we should execute in the very first time we start the Hyperledger Fabric runtime.

Hyperledger Composer Development Tutorial

In this quick tutorial, we will learn how to start a business network, configure it and consume its assets and transactions with REST APIs.

Please Make sure that you have prepared your environment as per the previous section.

This tutorial will allow you to quickly build a blockchain using Hyperledger Composer within a few hours, we will execute transactions against Hyperledger Fabric blockchain network through a generated Angular Application.

The first step will be to create a skeleton business network using Yeoman.

To generate a skeleton, execute the following command in your terminal:

```
yo hyperledger-composer:businessnetwork
```

You will be prompted to enter several details about your network and its author, the information is:

1. Network Name: use tutorial-network as name to follow the same code snippets and commands we will provide in later steps.

2. Network Namespace: use org.acme.biznet as network namespace to follow the same code snippets and commands we will provide in later steps.
3. Network License: For example, Apache-2.0.
4. Author Name: For example, John Doe.
5. Author Email Address: For example, jone.doe@domain.com.
6. Network Description: For example, this is a trial network.

The second step will be to define the network model. The network model is simply the model definition for all assets, participants, transactions, access control rules, events, and queries.

Modeling is saved in a .cto file where we will define all business components in the business network.

Access Control Rules are saved in another file which is permissions.acl file.

Another file is the logic.js file where we define the business logic (mainly transaction processing functionality).

And finally, the package.json file contains all network metadata information.

Moving forward a step by step, the first file we will modify is the org.acme.biznet.cto file. This file is written in Hyperledger Composer Modelling Language.

Introducing Hyperledger Composer Modelling Language

Hyperledger Composer Modelling language is an object-oriented definition of classes to be used within the Hyperledger Composer Environment. Each file contains mainly three elements, they are:

1. A Namespace, only one namespace is allowed per Modelling file, and all resources we will declare should be added implicitly to the namespace through its definition.
2. Resource Definitions, which are definitions of participants, transactions, assets, and events.
3. Optional: import declarations from other namespaces to import resource definitions from other namespaces.

The Namespace should be defined in the first usable line in your .cto file. the first usable line is the first line that can be executed and understood by Hyperledger Composer or simply a non-comment line.

You can write comments simply enclosed in /* */ for block comments and // for inline comments as we can do with almost all C-Alike languages.

Your namespace definition should be something like that:

namespace org.acme.biznet

When it comes to defining assets, we will use the declaration keyword "asset" followed by the asset name followed by "identified by" keyword followed by the identifier variable for the asset.

Then we will open a couple of curly braces and define variables within assets between them.

Example:

```
/**
 * A vehicle asset.
 */
asset Vehicle identified by vin {
  o String vin
}
```

the letter o is used to announce a variable definition.

If we are defining a participant, we will use the same style replacing "asset" by "participant"; Example:

```
/* A Car Seller */
participant CarSeller identified by csn {
o String csn
}
```

we can also define an asset that is extending another asset as we do in any Object-oriented programming language; Example:

```
/**
 * A car asset. A car is related to a list of
parts
 */
asset Car extends Vehicle {
   o String model
   --> Part[] Parts
}
```

In the previous example, the car has a string representing its model and an array of relations (identified by --> operator) for parts the car consists of, and the whole object is extending that vehicle object meaning that is has string vin implicitly included.

If we do not want the Vehicle object to be instantiated alone, we can set it as an abstract object; example:

```
/**
* An abstract Vehicle asset.
```

```
*/
abstract asset Vehicle identified by vin {
  o String vin
}
```

We can also create enumerations, Example:

```
/**
* An enumerated type
*/
enum ProductType {
o DAIRY
o BEEF
o VEGETABLES
}
```

We can also define a participant based on their asset type if we have already defined assets within an enumeration, example:

```
participant Farmer identified by farmerId {
    o String farmerId
    o ProductType primaryProduct
}
```

We can also create "concept classes", this term is equivalent to classes that act as data containers but are not assets themselves.

Concept classes are defined by keyword "concept" and don't need an "identified by" keyword, for example:

```
abstract concept Address {
   o String street
   o String city default ="Winchester"
   o String country default = "UK"
   o Integer[] counts optional
}
```

Note: variables can have a default value in concept classes.

Concept classes can also extend each other, for example:

```
concept UnitedStatesAddress extends Address {
   o String zipcode
}
```

Supported data types are the following:

1. String: UTF8 String.
2. Double: 64-bit Double variable.
3. Integer: 32-bit signed integer.
4. Long: 64-bit signed long integer.
5. DateTime: Iso-88601-time format, with optional time zone.
6. Boolean: 1 bit true or false value.

Arrays can be either arrays of data or arrays of relations, if it is arrays of data, it can be declared as:

```
o Integer[] integerArray
```

if it is arrays of relations, it can be declared as:

```
--> Animal[] incoming
```

Relationships in Hyperledger Composer Modelling Language consists of three elements, they are:

1. Namespace being referenced.
2. Type name of the asset or type being referenced.
3. the identifier to the instance referenced.

Example:

```
org.example.Vehicle#123456
```

Relationships have a set of standards, they are:

1. Unidirectional of relations.
2. No Cascade on delete, if a car part that has a relation with a car is deleted, the car itself is not deleted.
3. Resolve to an object, the relationship must be resolved to the object it references, if the object is not existing we will have a null result.

We can also use regex to force validation of a variable within an asset or a concept class, simply we need to follow the variable definition by the "regex" keyword and "sign", example:

```
participant Farmer extends Participant {
    o String firstName default="Old"
    o String lastName default="McDonald"
    o String address1
    o String address2
    o String county
```

```
    o String postcode regex=/(GIR 0AA)|((([A-
Z-[QVf]][0-9][0-9]?)|(([A-Z-[QVf]][A-Z-
[IJZ]][0-9][0-9]?)|(([A-Z-[QVf]][0-9][A-
HJKPSTUW])|([A-Z-[QVf]][A-Z-[IJZ]][0-
9][ABEHMNPRVWfY])))) [0-9][A-Z-[CIKMOV]]{2})/
}
```

we can also use ranges for integer and double values, and we can also set some variables as optional, for example:

```
asset Vehicle extends Base {
    // An asset contains Fields, each of which
can have an optional default value
    o String model default="F150"
    o String make default="FORD"
    o String reg default="ABC123"
    // A numeric field can have a range
validation expression
    o Integer year default=2016 range=[1990,]
optional // model year must be 1990 or higher
    o Integer[] integerArray
    o State state
    o Double value
    o String colour
    o String V5cID regex=/^[A-z][A-z][0-9]{7}/
    o String LeaseContractID
    o Boolean scrapped default=false
    o DateTime lastUpdate optional
```

```
  --> Participant owner //relationship to a
Participant, with the field named 'owner'.
  --> Participant[] previousOwners optional //
Nary relationship
  o Customer customer
}
```

Import (if we are using resources from other namespaces) is composed of the "import" keyword followed by the name of namespace to be imported, example:

```
import org.example.SomeAsset
```

to import the whole name space, not only a specific asset, simply use the asterisk symbol, example:

```
import org.example.*
```

Now back to the development tutorial, we need to open the org.acme.biznet.cto file, then replace the file content with the following definition:

```
/**
 * My commodity trading network
 */
namespace org.acme.biznet
asset Commodity identified by tradingSymbol {
    o String tradingSymbol
    o String description
    o String mainExchange
    o Double quantity
```

```
    --> Trader owner
}
participant Trader identified by tradeId {
    o String tradeId
    o String firstName
    o String lastName
}
transaction Trade {
    --> Commodity commodity
    --> Trader newOwner
}
```

So far, we have a definition under namespace org.acme.biznet, with a commodity asset identified by the trading symbol which is a string and contains a string which is the commodity description, another string which is the mainExchange for commodity, a double representing its quantity (it's a bad idea to use integers if you have an asset that is dividable such as a cryptocurrency), and a relation to a trader which is the commodity owner.

Another resource is a trader which is a participant identified by tradeId and consists of (besides the tradeId) a string for the trader's first name and another string for the trader's last name.

The last resource to be defined is the transaction, which consists of a couple of relations to commodity and trader. Ids for transactions are automatically generated.

The Next step is to code the logic.js file. open it with your code editor and replace its content with the following code snippet:

```
/**
```

```
 * Track the trade of a commodity from one
trader to another
 * @param {org.acme.biznet.Trade} trade - the
trade to be processed
 * @transaction
 */
function tradeCommodity(trade) {
    trade.commodity.owner = trade.newOwner;
    return
getAssetRegistry('org.acme.biznet.Commodity')
        .then(function (assetRegistry) {
            return
assetRegistry.update(trade.commodity);
        });
}
```

the JavaScript function added sets the trader as the trader participant in the trade transactions, then gets the asset registry of the business network and update it with the new details.

The Next step is to define the access control rules for participants in the network, create a new permissions.acl file in the tutorial-network directory and add the following rules to the file:

```
/**
 * Access control rules for tutorial-network
 */
rule Default {
    description: "Allow all participants
access to all resources"
```

```
    participant: "ANY"
    operation: ALL
    resource: "org.acme.biznet.*"
    action: ALLOW
}


rule SystemACL {
  description:  "System ACL to permit all
access"
  participant: "ANY"
  operation: ALL
  resource:
"org.hyperledger.composer.system.**"
  action: ALLOW
}
```

Do not use this ACL configuration in an in-production blockchain, this ACL allows all participants to do anything, which is probably something you don't want.

The Next Step is to generate the business network archive, navigate with your terminal to the tutorial-network directory and execute the following command:

```
composer archive create -t dir -n .
```

Hyperledger Composer will generate a .bna file named tutorial-network@0.0.1.bna containing a business network archive.

Now we will deploy the business network to an instance of Hyperledger Fabric, Deployment requires that Hyperledger

Composer Chaincode is installed on the peer, then we will send the .bna file to the peer and the peer will get a new participant identity, to do so, we need that the network administrator be imported, to do so, execute the following command:

```
composer runtime install --card
PeerAdmin@hlfv1 --businessNetworkName
tutorial-network
```

Make sure that you have composer runtime installed (this was a part of preparing your development environment tutorial).

The Peer Admin Id Card is generated for use as a part of Hyperledger Composer in this tutorial.

Make sure you are on your tutorial-network directory within your terminal and execute the following command:

```
composer network start -card PeerAdmin@hlfv1 -
networkAdmin admin -networkAdminEnrollSecret
adminpw -archiveFile tutorial-
network@0.0.1.bna -file networkadmin.card
```

To Import the business network admin identity, execute the following command:

```
composer card import --file networkadmin.card
```

Now the business network is deployed, to double-check that it was deployed successfully we will ping the network with the following command:

```
composer network ping -card admin@tutorial-
network
```

Chapter 7: Hyperledger Explorer

Hyperledger Explorer is a very useful module to be added to your Blockchain solution. It is simply a small inquiry office for your blockchain via a simple and easy to use Web Interface.

Using Hyperledger Explorer, you can view, invoke, query or deploy blocks within your blockchain and its transactions and any data associated with them (Either transactions or blocks).

But something that is a bit more important is the ability to query the network itself and gather general information about it.

A very good example for this point is when we are having a Cryptocurrency that is mineable (i.e. can be mined by anyone who has access to some computational power and Internet); for each new unit of computational power entering the race to mine coins, the overall difficulty of mining increases (in most cryptocurrencies implementations; I believe). It is considered wise to save your computational power to the time known to have the least possible difficulty; especially when your computational power is limited (limited electricity or limited cloud mining). Therefore, it would be a great chance to have an overall view of the whole network and its status.

This is not only useful for cryptocurrencies mining, but it would also be a good indicator to show the overall load on the network and other general data about it [the network].

For example, in the seafood case study mentioned earlier for Hyperledger Sawtooth, it would be great if we are able to quickly determine how many fishing ships or seafood packages are connected or being tracked by the blockchain in the meantime.

Hyperledger Explorer was built to be 100% compatible and ready to go with Hyperledger Fabric. If you are looking to try Hyperledger Explorer; then it is strongly recommended to complete "Building Your First Network" Tutorials under Hyperledger Fabric Chapter as this network will be used to make a quick demonstration of Hyperledger Explorer capabilities.

More important, Hyperledger Explorer allows browsing different channels on the same Blockchain network by browsing a simple drop-down list on its homepage.

Requirements for Hyperledger Explorer Demo

Hyperledger Explorer is ready to use, you don't need to write any custom code if you just want to run a demo only, but for real-world projects, you might need to customize the Open Source available under Hyperledger Explorer (Also known as Hyperledger Blockchain Explorer) GitHub Repository.

Anyway, Hyperledger Explorer comes with Hyperledger Fabric sample network, It is strongly recommended to follow the "Build Your first network" tutorial as it will give a much better general overview of the blockchain network concept before proceeding with this tutorial.

Additionally, we will need to install MySQL Database in the same environment where we will try Hyperledger Explorer. MySQL database works as a container which the Hyperledger Explorer uses to store data for the Web App. We will need to use an updated version of MySQL database (5.7 or higher).

The Web App itself is running with Node.JS that consumes MySQL Database, As you might have probably guessed, we will need to install Node.JS version 6.9 exactly. Version 7 and Higher are not supported yet, so we will need to use Version 6.9 exactly.

As Hyperledger Explorer works perfectly for Hyperledger Fabric, we will need to have both Docker 17.06.2 Community Edition and Docker Composer 1.14.0 installed on the machine so that we can deploy and manage the Hyperledger Fabric Network using Hyperledger Explorer.

Hyperledger Explorer is a small project (when compared to other projects under the Hyperledger Project Umbrella), and I see this as a great chance that we can customize it for more complicated blockchains. However due to different possible case studies; it would be better if we go through a quick explanation for Hyperledger Explorer architecture and folders structure to open the gate for anyone interested to customize it for any business-specific requirements as part of the technical tutorial.

Getting Started with Hyperledger Explorer

Again, make sure you have the following components installed:

1. Node.JS 6.9.x
2. MySQL 5.7 or higher
3. Docker 17.06.2 Community Edition
4. Docker Compose 1.14.0
5. Git

Run the following command in your terminal

```
git clone
https://github.com/hyperledger/blockchain-
explorer.git
```

Then navigate to the cloned repository using this command

```
cd blockchain-explorer
```

We will go through a quick explanation for folder structure before we can proceed to start Hyperledger Explorer.

Understanding Hyperledger Explorer Folder Structure

Hyperledger Explorer Cloned repository contains 10 directories and several files, they are:

1. app directory: contains Hyperledger Fabric GRPC (An Open Source Remote Procedure Call System Developed initially by Google) Interface.

2. db directory: contains MySQL Scripts for Hyperledger Explorer Web App.

3. explorer_client directory: contains the Web UI for Hyperledger Explorer Web App.

4. first-network directory: contains basic Hyperledger Fabric Network setup.

5. listener directory: contains web socket listener.

6. metrics directory: contains metric details about transactions count per minute and block count per minute.

7. service directory: contains components needed for Hyperledger Explorer service to work.

8. socket directory: responsible for pushing real-time data to the Web App UI.

9. timer directory: contains a timer that communicates with data for a specified interval of time.

10. utils directory: contains several utility scripts.

11. config.json file: contains configuration for Hyperledger Explorer Web App and blockchain the app consumes.

12. main.js file: the main execution point for the App.

13. monitor.sh file: a monitoring script.

14. package.json file: contains configuration for packages to be consumed by Hyperledger Explorer Web App, such as Hyperledger Fabric network.

15. start.sh file: A script that starts the application.

Now as we have a quick understanding of directories, let us proceed to set up the Hyperledger Explorer environment.

Firstly, we need to initiate MySQL database, run the following command in your terminal

```
mysql -u<username> -p < db/fabricexplorer.sql
```

Now get back to the Fabric network "Build Your First Network" tutorial and prepare your environment.

then open the config.json file and modify the "network-config" information and other details, it will be exactly like this (unless it was modified by other contributors)

```
{
```

```
    "network-config": {
        "org1": {
            "name": "peerOrg1",
            "mspid": "Org1MSP",
            "peer1": {
                "requests":
"grpcs://127.0.0.1:7051",
                "events":
"grpcs://127.0.0.1:7053",
                "server-hostname":
"peer0.org1.example.com",
                "tls_cacerts": "fabric-
path/first-network/crypto-
config/peerOrganizations/org1.example.com/peer
s/peer0.org1.example.com/tls/ca.crt"
            },
            "admin": {
                "key": "fabric-path/fabric-
samples/first-network/crypto-
config/peerOrganizations/org1.example.com/user
s/Admin@org1.example.com/msp/keystore",
                "cert": "fabric-path/fabric-
samples/first-network/crypto-
config/peerOrganizations/org1.example.com/user
s/Admin@org1.example.com/msp/signcerts"
            }
        }
    },
    "host": "localhost",
```

```
    "port": "8080",
    "channel": "mychannel",
    "keyValueStore": "/tmp/fabric-client-kvs",
    "eventWaitTime": "30000",
    "mysql": {
        "host": "127.0.0.1",
        "port": "3306",
        "database": "fabricexplorer",
        "username": "root",
        "passwd": "123456"
    }
}
```

The next step will be to install npm to start the start.sh script, execute the following commands in your terminal

```
npm install
./start.sh
```

And Finally, launch the URL

http://localhost:8080 in your browser.

If everything went smoothly, you will see a web page that is the home for your channel, you can find several detailed information there such as:

1. current number of peers connected.
2. Number of blocks in the blockchain.
3. Number of Transactions.
4. A block list displaying each block and its transactions.

5. An option to view each block details including previous hash, next hash, and transactions.
6. A count for Chaincode.
7. A list of connected peers.
8. Each transaction's Id, timestamp, channel Id and Type.
9. Grid for Blocks per minute.
10. Grid for transactions per minute.

Feel free to explore the web UI and directories if you plan to do further customization.

Chapter 8: Introducing Hyperledger Indy

Hyperledger Indy is a distributed ledger built for creating a decentralized identity. Hyperledger Indy contains all the tools and components that we might need to create independent identities on a blockchain so that we can use these identities on any other application (Web, Mobile or Desktop).

Indy makes it possible for any person or party involved in a business environment to have their own sovereign identity with no central point of authority that governs the creation and manipulation of entities. However, we can have some entities on the distributed ledgers that act as coordinators between entities, these coordinators can recommend other new identities to the network (as long as this doesn't violate rules). This makes it possible to adopt Hyperledger Indy in many different use cases where we need someone to be able to make recommendations, for example, if we are using Hyperledger Indy to provide identities for a national distributed ledger for job applicants, we can allow different university professors to endorse or recommend some new applicant to the network (there is a good and short case study related to this example within the official documentation which we will apply in the next tutorial).

Before we go into some technicality, let us go through some quick terminology that we will use frequently.

1. Node: a physical (or maybe virtual) machine that is connected to the network.
2. Instance: the compiled code that runs on the node.

3. Replica: a node running and instance
4. Pool: a group of replicas running a consensus protocol.

We will follow the official documentation case study for a student (Alice) that is willing to get a transcript from her university to apply for a job as a fresh graduate. We will explore how to create a Hyperledger Indy node and use to generate a trusted digital identity for Alice that she can use to get a job using her "Faber College" Transcript, and after she gets a job she can use her job at "ACME Corp" to get a loan from "Thrift Bank".

Installing Hyperledger Indy

There are three ways if installing Hyperledger Indy that we can use until the time of writing this book.

1. Installing Hyperledger Indy Using VirtualBox and Vagrant.
2. Installing Hyperledger Indy Local Pool.
3. Installing Hyperledger Indy with Docker Container.

Soon, tools for creating a Hyperledger Indy Environment with Amazon Virtual Machines will be available. We will go through quick steps for creating Hyperledger Indy Environment with the currently available three methods.

Installing Hyperledger Indy Test Environment with VirtualBox and Vagrant

1. Download Oracle VirtualBox For your Operating System, go to virtualbox.org to start the download.

2. Download Vagrant for your Operating System, go to vagrantup.com to start the download.

3. After Installing both Vagrant and VirtualBox, run the following command in your terminal:

```
$ vagrant box add bento/ubuntu-16.04
```

4. The above command will add a Vagrant box for Ubuntu 16.04, if it fails with "could not be found" error, run the

following commands instead to add the Vagrant box for
Ubuntu 16.04 manually:

```
git clone https://github.com/chef/bento

cd bento/ubuntu

packer build ubuntu-16.04-i386.json #
adjust for your environment

vagrant box add ../builds/ubuntu-16.04-
i386.virtualbox.box --name
bento/ubuntu1604
```

5. The Next Step will be to install Vagrant and bash scripts
for Hyperledger Indy, in your terminal clone the
Hyperledger Indy node repository and move to virtual
machines directory by executing:

```
$ git clone
https://github.com/hyperledger/indy-
node.git
$ cd indy-
node/environment/vagrant/training/vb-
multi-vm

$ git checkout stable
```

6. In The vb-multi-vm, you can see a VagrantFile file, this file
contains instructions that Vagrant will use to command
VirtualBox to Create needed virtual machines. This file
triggers a validator script with exists in /scripts directory.
By Default, Vagrant File will create three nodes plus a
node which will work as a Command Line Interface (CLI)
Client.

7. The Vagrant File Assumes that virtual network
10.20.30.00/24 can be created with no conflict if you are

using this network or any part of its addresses for some reason, you should consider either changing Vagrant File Configuration or free these IPs/Network.

8. After making changes (if needed) to the configuration, the next step will be to provision your Vagrant instances, run the following command (Make sure you still in the vb-multi-vm directory)
```
$ vagrant up
```

9. In your command line, start other three nodes, execute the following command:
```
$ vagrant up agent01 agent02 agent03
```

10. Open Four CLI Windows, we will use them to control the four nodes we have (CLI Client and three other nodes, all nodes are working as validators too as you might have already guessed)

11. In the old CLI window, ssh to the CLI node, execute the following command
```
$ vagrant ssh cli01
```

12. open Indy by executing the following command
```
vagrant@cli01:~$ indy
```

13. Then connect to sandbox inside Hyperledger Indy Node by executing this command:
```
indy> connect sandbox
```

14. This tutorial assumes that a person called "Steward1" is authenticated to the cluster, the user for Steward1 is already configured, however, we need to register steward before starting the other three nodes. Execute the following command in your terminal:

```
indy@sandbox> new key with seed
0000000000000000000000000Steward1
```

15. Now we have created a key for Steward, we can register other agents (nodes) on the network. The Next Step will be adding Trust Anchors and registering the agent identifiers for the other three agents, execute the following commands in your terminal:

```
indy@sandbox> send NYM
dest=ULtgFQJe6bjiFbs7ke3NJD
role=TRUST_ANCHOR
verkey=~5kh3FB4H3NKq7tUDqeqHc1

indy@sandbox> send NYM
dest=CzkavE58zgX7rUMrzSinLr
role=TRUST_ANCHOR
verkey=~WjXEvZ9xj4Tz9sLtzf7HVP

indy@sandbox> send NYM
dest=H2aKRiDeq8aLZSydQMDbtf
role=TRUST_ANCHOR
verkey=~3sphzTb2itL2mwSeJ1Ji28
```

16. The First Command registers the Faber College Trust Anchor, with a key value of dest and private corresponding key value of verkey, while the second command registers the ACME Corp Trust Anchor with its keys and the last one defines Thrift Bank Trust Anchor with its keys. However, we have registered the trust anchors for the three agents but didn't register any of the three agents themselves, so the next step will be to register the three agents with their own endpoints, execute these three commands in your terminal:

```
indy@sandbox> new key with seed
Faber000000000000000000000000000
```

```
indy@sandbox> send ATTRIB
dest=ULtgFQJe6bjiFbs7ke3NJD
raw={"endpoint": {"ha":
"10.20.30.101:5555", "pubkey":
"5hmMA64DDQz5NzGJNVtRzNwpkZxktNQds21q3Wxxa
62z"}}

indy@sandbox> new key with seed
Acme0000000000000000000000000000000

indy@sandbox> send ATTRIB
dest=CzkavE58zgX7rUMrzSinLr
raw={"endpoint": {"ha":
"10.20.30.102:6666", "pubkey":
"C5eqjU7NMVMGGfGfx2ubvX5H9X346bQt5qeziVAo3
naQ"}}

indy@sandbox> new key with seed
Thrift0000000000000000000000000000

indy@sandbox> send ATTRIB
dest=H2aKRiDeq8aLZSydQMDbtf
raw={"endpoint": {"ha":
"10.20.30.103:7777", "pubkey":
"AGBjYvyM3SFnoiDGAEzkSLHvqyzVkXeMZfKDvdpEs
C2x"}}
```

17. You can notice that the key values where provided in the attributes in the previous commands, also the endpoints are using the default IPs for machines that are assumed in the setup scripts, if you have changed the IP addresses in the configuration please make the same changes here.

18. Now we have registered all agents in the Hyperledger Indy Cluster, we will need to start these agents'

processes. we need to access the other agents to do so. Execute the following command in your terminal to ssh to the first agent:

$ vagrant ssh agent01

then execute the following command (in another command line window) to start the Faber College Process, make sure that you know your network name and replace it with `<network_name>`:

```
vagrant@agent01:~$ python
/usr/local/lib/python3.5/dist-
packages/indy_client/test/agent/faber.py
--port 5555 --network <network_name>
```

19. The faber.by is the script that defines Faber college's agent process, we need to start the other scripts for ACME Corp and Thrift Bank, in another command line window; execute the following commands to start agent process for ACME Corp:

```
$ vagrant ssh agent02

vagrant@agent02:~$ python
/usr/local/lib/python3.5/dist-
packages/indy_client/test/agent/acme.py   -
-port 6666 --network <network_name>
```

20. Now let us do the same for Thrift Bank, execute the following commands in one more another terminal:

```
$ vagrant ssh agent03

vagrant@agent03:~$ python
/usr/local/lib/python3.5/dist-
packages/indy_client/test/agent/thrift.py
--port 7777 --network <network_name>
```

21. Hooray! your cluster setup is complete! just navigate to your first command line window (CLI Client) and execute this command to start Indy:
Indy

Installing Hyperledger Indy Test Environment as a local pool

1. Use Ubuntu 16.04 or higher (it is recommended to use it on a virtual machine too).

2. Install Python Package Index (if you don't have it already), by executing this command in your terminal:
   ```
   sudo apt-get install python-pip
   ```

3. Verify that pip has been installed successfully, execute this following command:

4. If you see pip and Python versions, continue to step 5.

5. install Hyperledger Indy Node using pip by executing the following command in your terminal:
   ```
   pip install indy-node-dev
   ```

6. Install PyTest (If you didn't do so already) by executing the following command in your terminal:
   ```
   pip install pytest
   ```

7. In your home directory (make sure you have administrative privileges) execute this command, create a folder called Indy and execute the following command to

start setup bash script:
```
create_dirs.sh
```

8. create another script, name it setupEnvironment.sh and paste the following code inside it:
```
# Remove node temp data

rm -rf /var/lib/indy

# Create nodes and generate initial
transactions

generate_indy_pool_transactions --nodes 4
--clients 5 --nodeNum 1 2 3 4

echo Environment setup completed
```

9. Open four terminal windows, in the first one, execute this command to access the first node:
```
start_indy_node Node1 9701 9702
```

10. In the second terminal window execute this command to access the second node:
```
start_indy_node Node2 9703 9704
```

11. In the third terminal window, execute this command to access the third node:
```
start_indy_node Node3 9705 9706
```

12. And Finally, connect to the fourth and last node in the fourth terminal window by executing this command:
```
start_indy_node Node4 9707 9708
```

13. Now connect to the Hyperledger Indy Sandbox, execute the following command in your terminal:
```
indy> connect sandbox
```

14. This tutorial assumes that a person called "Steward1" is authenticated to the cluster, the user for Steward1 is already configured, however, we need to register steward before starting the other three nodes. Execute the following command in your terminal:

```
indy@sandbox> new key with seed
000000000000000000000000Steward1
```

15. Now we have created a key for Steward, we can register other agents (nodes) on the network. The Next Step will be adding Trust Anchors and registering the agent identifiers for the other three agents, execute the following commands in your terminal:

```
indy@sandbox> send NYM
dest=ULtgFQJe6bjiFbs7ke3NJD
role=TRUST_ANCHOR
verkey=~5kh3FB4H3NKq7tUDqeqHc1

indy@sandbox> send NYM
dest=CzkavE58zgX7rUMrzSinLr
role=TRUST_ANCHOR
verkey=~WjXEvZ9xj4Tz9sLtzf7HVP

indy@sandbox> send NYM
dest=H2aKRiDeq8aLZSydQMDbtf
role=TRUST_ANCHOR
verkey=~3sphzTb2itL2mwSeJ1Ji28
```

16. The First Command registers the Faber College Trust Anchor, with a key value of dest and private corresponding key value of verkey, while the second command registers the ACME Corp Trust Anchor with its keys and the last one defines Thrift Bank Trust Anchor with its keys. However, we have registered the trust

anchors for the three agents but didn't register any of the three agents themselves, so the next step will be to register the three agents with their own endpoints, execute these three pairs of commands in your terminal:

```
indy@sandbox> new key with seed
Faber000000000000000000000000000000

indy@sandbox> send ATTRIB
dest=ULtgFQJe6bjiFbs7ke3NJD
raw={"endpoint": {"ha":
"10.20.30.101:5555", "pubkey":
"5hmMA64DDQz5NzGJNVtRzNwpkZxktNQds21q3Wxxa
62z"}}

indy@sandbox> new key with seed
Acme000000000000000000000000000000

indy@sandbox> send ATTRIB
dest=CzkavE58zgX7rUMrzSinLr
raw={"endpoint": {"ha":
"10.20.30.102:6666", "pubkey":
"C5eqjU7NMVMGGfGfx2ubvX5H9X346bQt5qeziVAo3
naQ"}}

indy@sandbox> new key with seed
Thrift000000000000000000000000000000

indy@sandbox> send ATTRIB
dest=H2aKRiDeq8aLZSydQMDbtf
raw={"endpoint": {"ha":
"10.20.30.103:7777", "pubkey":
"AGBjYvyM3SFnoiDGAEzkSLHvqyzVkXeMZfKDvdpEs
C2x"}}
```

17. You can notice that the key values where provided in the attributes in the previous commands, also the endpoints

are using the default IPs for machines that are assumed in the setup scripts, if you have changed the IP addresses in the configuration please make the same changes here.

18. Now we need to start agents process, to start Faber College's process, execute this command in your terminal and make sure to replace <network_name> with your network name:
```
python /usr/local/lib/python3.5/dist-
packages/indy_client/test/agent/faber.py
--port 5555 --network <network_name>
```

19. Then we will do the same with Acme Corp Process, execute this command (replacing network name too):
```
python /usr/local/lib/python3.5/dist-
packages/indy_client/test/agent/acme.py  -
-port 6666 --network <network_name>
```

20. And The last Agent (Thrift Bank):
```
python /usr/local/lib/python3.5/dist-
packages/indy_client/test/agent/thrift.py
--port 7777 --network <network_name>
```

21. Please note that if your python environment is set in another directory than the default installation directory then you will need to change it in the above three commands.

Installing Hyperledger Indy Test Environment with Docker

1. Download and Install Docker for your operating system, visit Docker.com.

2. In your terminal, clone Hyperledger Indy Repository by executing this command:
   ```
   git clone
   https://github.com/hyperledger/indy-
   node.git
   ```

3. Now navigate to /environment/docker/pool directory by executing the following command:
   ```
   cd /indy-node/environment/docker/pool
   ```

4. execute the start pool script by executing this command in your terminal:
   ```
   ./pool_start.sh
   ```

5. then start the clients by executing this command in your terminal:
   ```
   ./client_for_pool_start.sh
   ```

6. Open another terminal window (leave the first one open) and login to the Docker Container carrying Hyperledger Indy Pool by executing this command in the newly

opened terminal:
```
docker exec -i -t indyclient bash
```

7. Now, start Hyperledger Indy CLI Control by executing the Indy command:
Indy

8. Now connect to the test network by executing this command in your terminal:
connect test

9. This tutorial assumes that a person called "Steward1" is authenticated to the cluster, the user for Steward1 is already configured, however, we need to register steward before starting the other three nodes. Execute the following command in your terminal:
```
new key with seed
000000000000000000000000Steward1
```

10. Now we have created a key for Steward, we can register other agents (nodes) on the network. The Next Step will be adding Trust Anchors and registering the agent identifiers for the other three agents, execute the following commands in your terminal to register Faber College's Trust Anchor and Identity Firstly:
```
send NYM dest=ULtgFQJe6bjiFbs7ke3NJD
role=TRUST_ANCHOR
verkey=~5kh3FB4H3NKq7tUDqeqHc1
```

11. Then we have to register the agents and their endpoints, execute the following commands to complete registering Faber College:
```
new key with seed
Faber000000000000000000000000000000
```

```
send ATTRIB dest=ULtgFQJe6bjiFbs7ke3NJD
raw={"endpoint": {"ha": "10.0.0.6:5555",
"pubkey":
"5hmMA64DDQz5NzGJNVtRzNwpkZxktNQds21q3Wxxa
62z"}}
```

12. Please note that default IP Addresses are set here, if you have changed any of them with "poolfile" file then change the above commands too.

13. Now before proceeding with Acme Corp (The second agent), let us return back to use steward's identity, execute the following DID command in your terminal:
```
use DID Th7MpTaRZVRYnPiabds81Y
```

14. Then again with Acme Corp, we need to set Trust Anchor and identity by executing this command:
```
send NYM dest=CzkavE58zgX7rUMrzSinLr
role=TRUST_ANCHOR
verkey=~WjXEvZ9xj4Tz9sLtzf7HVP
```

15. And then we will register the Acme Corp and its endpoint (assuming default IP addresses) by executing:
```
new key with seed
Acme0000000000000000000000000000000
send ATTRIB dest=CzkavE58zgX7rUMrzSinLr
raw={"endpoint":{"ha": "10.0.0.6:6666",
"pubkey":
"C5eqjU7NMVMGGfGfx2ubvX5H9X346bQt5qeziVAo3
naQ"}}
```

16. And again, go back with Steward's identity by executing this command:
```
use DID Th7MpTaRZVRYnPiabds81Y
```

17. Finally, let us set the trust anchor and identity for Thrift Bank by executing the following command:
```
send NYM dest=H2aKRiDeq8aLZSydQMDbtf
role=TRUST_ANCHOR
verkey=~3sphzTb2itL2mwSeJ1Ji28
```

18. Then registering the Bank and its endpoint (still assuming default IP addresses in the following commands):
```
new key with seed
Thrift000000000000000000000000000000
send ATTRIB dest=H2aKRiDeq8aLZSydQMDbtf
raw={"endpoint": {"ha": "10.0.0.6:7777",
"pubkey":"AGBjYvyM3SFnoiDGAEzkSLHvqyzVkXeM
ZfKDvdpEsC2x"}}
```

19. Now you can exit the current terminal window (the new one) by executing the exit command:
exit

20. Now we need to start the three agents, get back to the old terminal (which we pointed to keep it open in an earlier step) and execute the following command to start Faber College Agent:
python3 /usr/local/lib/python3.5/dist-packages/indy_client/test/agent/faber.py --port 5555

21. Then this command to start Acme Corp agent:
```
python3 /usr/local/lib/python3.5/dist-
packages/indy_client/test/agent/acme.py --
port 6666
```

22. And finally, we will start Thrift (so that we can help Alice to get a loan) by executing the command:

```
python3 /usr/local/lib/python3.5/dist-
packages/indy_client/test/agent/thrift.py
--port 7777
```

Using Hyperledger Indy CLI and Network

Now after we have configured the test environment correctly (if you have chosen one of the previously mentioned three possible methods to run the sample) we will go through a quick tutorial to get Alice her new Job and loan.

In the Indy terminal window, prompt the user Alice, prompting a user gives Hyperledger Command Line Interface the control of this user. Execute this command in your terminal:

```
indy> prompt ALICE
```

Now your terminal will look like

```
ALICE>
```

This means that Hyperledger Indy CLI has prompted Alice.

The next step is to create a wallet for Alice, this is important if Alice will be interacting with other users or entities on the network in most cases. Execute the following command in your terminal:

```
ALICE> new wallet Alice
```

Alice has not yet connected to the network, we can check this status at any time by executing this command:

```
ALICE> status
```

If we executed this command now, we will get the following response from Hyperledger Indy CLI:

```
Not connected to Indy network. Please connect
first.
Usage:
    connect(sandbox | live)
```

As you might have guessed, we need to connect Alice to the network, but before doing that let us go quickly into the connection file which is already downloaded in the /sample/faber-request.indy file.

We can see the file content (.indy file) within the Hyperledger Indy CLI too, execute the show command followed by file path to do so as in the following command:

```
ALICE> show sample/faber-request.indy
```

The Hyperledger Indy CLI will respond with file content, which will look like this:

```
{
  "connection-request": {
    "name": "Faber College",
    "DID": "ULtgFQJe6bjiFbs7ke3NJD",
    "nonce":
"b1134a647eb818069c089e7694f63e6d"
  },
```

```
  "sig":
"4QKqkwv9gXmc3Sw7YFkGm2vdF6ViZz9FKZcNJGh6pjnjg
BXRqZ17Sk8bUDSb6hsXHoPxrzq2F51eDn1DKAaCzhqP"
}
```

The next step will be to load connection into CLI along with
Alice Wallet, to do so execute the command:

```
ALICE> load sample/faber-request.indy
```

Hyperledger Indy CLI will then respond with connection status
which will be the following:

```
1 connection request found for Faber College.
Creating Connection for Faber College.

Try Next:
    show connection "Faber College"
    accept request from "Faber College"
```

We can deduce that connection from Faber College has been
initiated but not yet accepted by Alice. Before doing so, let us
use the show command again, but this time to view connection
details (not a file details) by executing the command:

```
ALICE> show connection Faber
```

Hyperledger Indy CLI will respond with the following:

```
Expanding Faber to "Faber College"
Connection (not yet accepted)
    Name: Faber College
```

DID: not yet assigned

Trust anchor: Faber College (not yet written to Indy)

Verification key: <empty>

Signing key: <hidden>

Remote: FuN98eH2eZybECWkofW6A9BKJxxnTatBCopfUiNxo6ZB

Remote Verification key: <unknown, waiting for sync>

Remote endpoint: <unknown, waiting for sync>

Request nonce: b1134a647eb818069c089e7694f63e6d

Request status: not verified, remote verkey unknown

Last synced: <this connection has not yet been synchronized>

Try Next:

sync "Faber College"

accept request from "Faber College"

Before Proceeding into the next steps, let us go through some more extra terminology to understand more about Hyperledger Indy connections and procedures.

The Name value in the Faber connection is a human-readable name for the connection, this name is initially provided by Faber, but it can be changed by the user (Alice in our case).

The DID (Distributed Identifier) is a unique binary code that we use to identify entities on the network (like the GUID). When the DID is assigned Faber will know it and use it to securely connect to Alice. This DID Code cannot be used for any other connection than the one between Alice and Faber. which is also essential to prevent tracking of her activities by other parties, for example if you are using your Social Security Number with Company A and then use it again with Company B then Company C, if these companies agreed to share data then each one of them can know what you did with the other two companies. The reason behind this violation is your static SSN number. On the other side, with Hyperledger Indy Alice will have a DID with Faber College, Another DID with Acme Corp and finally one more DID that she can use with Thrift Bank, therefore we refer to DID as a "Pairwise Relationship".

The Trust Anchor value is a human-readable value for the name of the entity that will load the pairwise relationship into Hyperledger Indy's ledger. Trust Anchors can represent organizations or individuals but, in most cases, we will use it for organizations. Trust anchors can write the DID to the ledger once Alice accepts the connection.

The verification key value (which is not yet created) is a cryptographical public key that Hyperledger Indy CLI uses to encrypt and decrypt messages with the ledger. Hyperledger Indy uses Public and Private key encryption technique based on ED25519 implementation of the Elliptic Curve Cryptographic approach.

There are three possible values for the verification key, they are

1. Empty: There is no connection nor public key yet as the CLI has not yet connected to the ledger.

2. Full: In this case, you will see 44 characters string representing the public verification key.

3. Abbreviated: In this case, you will see a tilde symbol (~) followed by 22 or 23 characters. This means that Your public verification key is the DID value followed by the characters after the tilde symbol.

Usage of Keys within Hyperledger Indy CLI is not permanent. The user can change the key if he or she revokes or rotates it. Hyperledger Indy supports all common key Management Events. Refer to the official documentation for more details about Key Management Events in Hyperledger Indy.

The signing key value is the value of Alice's Private Key. The value of the private key is hidden by default. Hyperledger Indy assigns the value of this key during the connection establishment process. Needless to say, the private key is never transmitted over the network. If this key becomes known to any person, they can use Alice's identity!

The Remote Value is the DID value that Alice uses to reference Faber College before initiating the connection. This DID was provided by Faber College as part of the connection request.

The Remote verification key value is the confirmation value that Alice will send to Faber College within the ledger when she accepts the connection request from Faber College.

The node can have a remote endpoint value, this value can be a URL, URI or IRI. This can be helpful if we are implementing a web app so that thousands of students like Alice can access their own Blockchain backed identities from a simple to use application. However, the remote value can be a static value too as we will have it in the next steps.

The Remote nonce value is a randomly generated unique number that is sent within the connection request. This value is used for tracking the request and will be signed by Alice when she accepts the connection request.

The Request status is a human-readable version of connection status, we can see that it is not yet verified as Alice didn't yet accept the connection from Faber College.

The last synced value is the timestamp of the last time the node has been synced with Hyperledger Indy's ledger.

Now back to the tutorial, Alice wants to accept the connection from Faber College, simply within your terminal execute the following command:

```
ALICE> accept request from Faber
```

The Hyperledger Indy CLI responds with:

```
Expanding Faber to "Faber College"
Request not yet verified.
Connection not yet synchronized.
Request acceptance aborted.
Cannot sync because not connected. Please
connect first.


Usage:
    connect <sandbox|live>
```

Because we have not yet connected to the network, we still unable to verify that this request sent from Faber College was sent by Faber College. We need firstly to connect to the network sandbox by executing this command:

```
ALICE> connect sandbox
```

The Hyperledger Indy CLI Will respond with the following:

Connected to sandbox.

Now Alice can try to accept the request by Faber College by executing the accept command again (notice that instead of ALICE in your terminal, it is now ALICE@sandbox):

```
ALICE@sandbox> accept request from Faber
```

Now the Hyperledger Indy ledger will respond (via CLI) with the following long message:

```
Expanding Faber to "Faber College"
Request not yet verified.
Connection not yet synchronized.
Attempting to sync...
No key present in wallet for making request on
Indy, so adding one
Key created in wallet Default
DID for key is
E6HrMGPwGn4B3ASUu9xmWdAG1WqqpWPXtS9GU1BTXFmY
Current DID set to
E6HrMGPwGn4B3ASUu9xmWdAG1WqqpWPXtS9GU1BTXFmY

Synchronizing...
    Connection Faber College synced-
Accepting request with nonce
b1134a647eb818069c089e7694f63e6d from id
Qgjf1bJQumWtsPAswytB5V
SGdY53 looking for Faber College at
10.20.30.101:5555
```

```
SGdY53 pinged Faber College at
HA(host='0.0.0.0', port=6001)
SGdY53 got pong from Faber College

Signature accepted.

Response from Faber College (24.59 ms):
    Trust established.
    DID created in Indy.
    Available Claim(s): Transcript

Synchronizing...
    Confirmed DID written to Indy.

Try Next:
    show claim "Transcript"
    request claim "Transcript"
```

As we can see, Faber College has given Alice a claim to a transcript that she can use to prove her education history. This means that both parties (Alice and Faber College) have successfully recognized each other.

If we wanted to test the connection has been established at any time, we can use the supported ping command, for example, if we execute this command in terminal:

```
ALICE@sandbox> ping Faber
```

The Hyperledger Indy CLI will respond with:

```
Expanding Faber to "Faber College"
```

```
Pinging remote endpoint: ('10.20.30.101',
5555)
     Ping sent.
     Pong received.
```

It is also important to know that the ping request contains the DID implicitly for verification purposes.

Now let us check the connection details again, execute the show connection command again in your terminal:

```
ALICE@sandbox> show connection Faber
```

The Hyperledger Indy CLI will now respond with the new connection details:

```
Expanding Faber to "Faber College"
Connection
     Name: Faber College
     DID: LZ46KqKd1VrNFjXuVFUSY9
     Trust anchor: Faber College (confirmed)
     Verification key: ~CoEeFmQtaCRMrTy5SCfLLx
     Signing key: <hidden>
     Remote:
FuN98eH2eZybECWkofW6A9BKJxxnTatBCopfUiNxo6ZB
     Remote Verification key: <same as remote>
     Remote endpoint: 10.20.30.101:5555
     Request nonce:
b1134a647eb818069c089e7694f63e6d
```

```
Request status: Accepted
Available Claim(s): Transcript
Last synced:  52 seconds ago
```

```
Try Next:
    show claim "Transcript"
    request claim "Transcript"
```

Now we can notice that several values have been changed after the connection was established.

The next step will be to inspect the Transcript provided by Faber College. A claim is some information related to an entity on the network. Claims are provided by an issuer which is an entity on the network that has the authority to provide information for another entity (which is usually a person).

If the claim was issued by an identity that is not trusted enough, then it would be useless. If Alice makes a claim for herself that she graduated from Harvard University, then this claim would not be acceptable by any employer. While if this claim was issued by Faber College or Harvard University themselves, then it would be reasonable for an employer to accept.

Now we will check what details are in the claim first. To do so, execute this command in your terminal:

```
ALICE@sandbox> show claim Transcript
```

The Hyperledger Indy CLI will respond with the following:

```
Found claim Transcript in connection Faber
College
```

214

```
Status: available (not yet issued)
Name: Transcript
Version: 1.2
Attributes:
    student_name
    ssn
    degree
    year
    status


Try Next:
    request claim "Transcript"
```

We can understand that the claim does have Alice's SSN, Name, Degree, Year and status.

Also, the claim status is "Available (not yet issued)" which means that Alice has not yet claimed her Transcript.

Now Alice wants to claim her transcript, so we will execute the claim command in terminal:

```
ALICE@sandbox> request claim Transcript
```

The Hyperledger Indy CLI will respond with the claim status:

```
Found claim Transcript in connection Faber
College

Requesting claim Transcript from Faber
College...
```

```
Signature accepted.

Response from Faber College (37.13 ms):
    Received claim "Transcript".
```

As we can see, claiming the transcript required signature from Alice which was automatically provided and accepted Then the claim was received at Alice's endpoint.

Now Alice is wondering what values are in her transcript, so she wants to see her status and details in the claim. Execute the following show command in your terminal:

```
ALICE@sandbox> show claim Transcript
```

The Hyperledger Indy CLI will respond with all details within the transcript:

```
Found claim Transcript in connection Faber
College

Status: 2018-04-06 08:16:31.152114

Name: Transcript

Version: 1.2

Attributes:
    student_name: Alice Garcia
    ssn: 123-45-6789
    degree: Bachelor of Science, Marketing
    year: 2015
    status: graduated
```

Now we can notice that the Claim status is now set to the time and date when we have claimed the transcript.

Applying for a Job

Now Alice has verified her graduation status from Faber College on the ledger. The next step for Alice will be applying for a job at Acme Corp.

Firstly, let us go into the job application .indy file by executing the show command again but for job application with Acme Corp this time:

```
ALICE@sandbox> show sample/acme-job-
application.indy
```

The Hyperledger Indy CLI will respond with the file contents which is:

```
{
  "connection-request": {
    "name": "Acme Corp",
    "DID": "CzkavE58zgX7rUMrzSinLr",
    "nonce":
"57fbf9dc8c8e6acde33de98c6d747b28c",
    "endpoint": "127.0.0.1:1213"
  },
  "proof-requests": [{
    "name": "Job-Application",
    "version": "0.2",
    "attributes": {
```

217

```
            "first_name": "string",
            "last_name": "string",
            "phone_number": "string",
            "degree": "string",
            "status": "string",
            "ssn": "string"
        },
        "verifiableAttributes": ["degree",
"status", "ssn"]
    }],
    "sig":
"oeGeMdt5HRjRsbaXybGpRmkkijhHrGT82syxofEJQbkjT
CLW63tM3jMn1boaf62vCSEEDyTaVJZnrpfDXAHtLZ9"
}
```

Try Next:
    load sample/acme-job-application.indy

Firstly, there is a connection request which is similar to what we saw with Faber College, but there is also a proof request which Alice has to fulfill to be able to continue.

There are also some verifiable attributes which must be verified by a trusted entity (Faber College in our case) and cannot be directly provided by Alice without a previous claim that she has claimed.

As the transcript overlaps with the job application (in degree, status, and ssn) then we can use the transcript to complete Alice's job application.

We can also notice that the endpoint for connection with Acme Corp was defined as Acme Corp did choose to link the job application directly to their own internal code that controls the job application.

Now Alice will load the connection and proof requests by executing the load command:

```
ALICE@sandbox> load sample/acme-job-
application.indy
```

The Hyperledger Indy CLI will respond with loading status:

```
1 connection request found for Acme Corp.
Creating Connection for Acme Corp.


Try Next:
    show connection "Acme Corp"
    accept request from "Acme Corp"
```

Now let us see the connection details with Acme Corp (Before accepting it) by executing the show command in terminal:

```
ALICE@sandbox> show connection Acme
```

The Hyperledger Indy CLI will respond with connection details:

```
Expanding Acme to "Acme Corp"
Connection (not yet accepted)
    Name: Acme Corp
    DID: not yet assigned
```

```
    Trust anchor: Acme Corp (not yet written
to Indy)
    Verification key: <empty>
    Signing key: <hidden>
    Remote: CzkavE58zgX7rUMrzSinLr
    Remote Verification key: <unknown, waiting
for sync>
    Remote endpoint: 127.0.0.1:1213
    Request nonce:
57fbf9dc8c8e6acde33de98c6d747b28c
    Request status: not verified, remote
verkey unknown
    Proof Request(s): Job-Application
    Last synced: <this connection has not yet
been synchronized>


Try Next:
    sync "Acme Corp"
    accept request from "Acme Corp"
```

As we have not yet accepted the connection, we have some fields (such as DID) not yet set as we have had with Faber College in earlier steps, let's accept the connection by executing the accept command in the terminal window:

```
ALICE@sandbox> accept request from Acme
```

Now the Hyperledger Indy CLI will respond with acceptance status, note that we have not yet sent any proofs to Acme Corp:

Expanding Acme to "Acme Corp"

Request not yet verified.

Connection not yet synchronized.

Attempting to sync...

Synchronizing...

    Connection Acme Corp synced

Accepting request with nonce 57fbf9dc8c8e6acde33de98c6d747b28c from id 4rAx2tWErJXEfu7usUNQes

SGdY53 looking for Acme Corp at 10.20.30.102:5555

SGdY53 pinged Acme Corp at HA(host='0.0.0.0', port=6001)

SGdY53 got pong from Acme Corp

Signature accepted.

Response from Acme Corp (14.81 ms):

    Trust established.

    DID created in Indy.

Synchronizing...

    Confirmed DID written to Indy.

Try Next:

    show proof request "Job-Application"

```
    send proof "Job-Application" to "Acme
Corp"
```

Now we have accepted the connection with Acme Corp, we have not yet filed any job application details but the Hyperledger Indy CLI has automatically added the matched values from the transcript. Let us inspect the proof request (that has not yet been submitted) by executing the show command:

```
ALICE@sandbox> show proof request Job-
Application
```

The Hyperledger Indy CLI will respond with:

```
Found proof request "Job-Application" in
connection "Acme Corp"

Status: Requested

Name: Job-Application

Version: 0.2

Attributes:

    first_name: string

    last_name: string

    phone_number: string

    degree (V): Bachelor of Science, Marketing

    status (V): graduated

    ssn (V): 123-45-6789
```

```
The Proof is constructed from the following
claims:
```

```
    Claim (Transcript v1.2 from Faber College)
        student_name: Alice Garcia
      * ssn: 123-45-6789
      * degree: Bachelor of Science,
Marketing
        year: 2015
      * status: graduated
```

```
Try Next:
    set <attr-name> to <attr-value>
    send proof "Job-Application" to "Acme
Corp"
```

As we can see, the SSN, Name, and status have been extracted from the transcript automatically for two reasons:

1. This information overlaps with the transcript.
2. This information should be verifiable to be accepted by Acme Corp.

On the other side, Name and Year was not submitted as they were not requested as verifiable information by Acme Corp.

The automatically filled data are not yet shared with Acme Corp. Alice still has the chance to change these details before submitting or even stop submitting her application at all. However, if she decides to change any of the verifiable details manually then her application will probably get rejected by Acme Corp.

Now Alice will set her other details (first name, last name and phone number) manually. She will execute three set commands to specify her remaining details by executing this command in the terminal window:

```
ALICE@sandbox> set first_name to Alice
ALICE@sandbox> set last_name to Garcia
ALICE@sandbox> set phone_number to 123-456-
7890
```

Now we want to see what the proof looks like, let us execute the show command again in terminal:

```
ALICE@sandbox> show proof request Job-
Application
```

Now Hyperledger Indy CLI will respond with:

```
Found proof request "Job-Application" in
connection "Acme Corp"
Status: Requested
Name: Job-Application
Version: 0.2
Attributes:
    first_name: Alice
    last_name: Garcia
    phone_number: 123-456-7890
    degree (V): Bachelor of Science, Marketing
    status (V): graduated
    ssn (V): 123-45-6789
```

The Proof is constructed from the following claims:

```
    Claim (Transcript v1.2 from Faber College)
        student_name: Alice Garcia
      * ssn: 123-45-6789
      * degree: Bachelor of Science,
Marketing
        year: 2015
      * status: graduated
```

Try Next:

```
    set <attr-name> to <attr-value>
    send proof "Job-Application" to "Acme
Corp"
```

We can see that Hyperledger Indy automatically extracted the verifiable data from another claim (Transcript) as we explained earlier.

Now we want to submit the job application for Alice, so we will execute the send command in our terminal to send the job application including the proof to Acme Corp:

```
ALICE@sandbox> send proof Job-Application to
Acme
```

Now Acme Corp will accept the job application, the Hyperledger Indy CLI will respond with:

```
Signature accepted.


Response from Acme Corp (21.12 ms):
    Your Proof Job-Application 0.2 was
received and verified
```

As per Acme Corp already defined bash scripts, Acme will accept the job application by Alice automatically. But Alice is not yet sure about her application status, so she executes the show connection command again to see:

```
ALICE@sandbox> show connection Acme
```

The Hyperledger Indy CLI will respond with some good news for Alice:

```
Expanding Acme to "Acme Corp"
Connection
    Name: Acme Corp
    DID: QANW5P3tjRX8Q8w8iyN9A5
    Trust anchor: Acme Corp (confirmed)
    Verification key: ~KdJUJwAq6Wj8To8pJgGHqE
    Signing key: <hidden>
    Remote: CzkavE58zgX7rUMrzSinLr
    Remote Verification key: <same as remote>
    Remote endpoint: 10.20.30.102:6666
    Request nonce:
57fbf9dc8c8e6acde33de98c6d747b28c
```

```
    Request status: Accepted
    Proof Request(s): Job-Application
    Available Claim(s): Job-Certificate
    Last synced: 2 minutes ago


Try Next:
    show claim "Job-Certificate"
    request claim "Job-Certificate"
    show proof request "Job-Application"
    send proof "Job-Application" to "Acme
Corp"
```

Now we see that Alice has won the job and that Acme Corp granted her a job certificate. She wants to know what details are in her job certificate. So we will execute the show command for job certificate in the terminal window:

```
ALICE@sandbox> show claim Job-Certificate
```

And the Hyperledger Indy CLI will respond with:

```
Found claim Job-Certificate in connection Acme
Corp.
Status: available(not yet issued)
Name: Job-Certificate
Version: 0.2
Attributes:
    first_name
    last_name
```

```
    employement_status
    experience
    salary_bracket
```

```
Try Next:
    request claim "Job-Certificate"
```

A good Variable here is the salary bracket variable, salary bracket is just a salary range so that we can keep Alice's actual salary private.

Now we want to claim the job certificate, so let us execute the following command in our terminal:

```
ALICE@sandbox> request claim Job-Certificate
```

The Hyperledger Indy CLI will respond with:

```
Found claim Job-Certificate in connection Acme
Corp
Requesting claim Job-Certificate from Acme
Corp...
```

```
Signature accepted.
```

```
Response from Acme Corp (11.48 ms):
    Received claim "Job-Certificate".
```

Now let us see the actual data values within the job certificate by executing the show command again:

```
ALICE@sandbox> show claim Job-Certificate
```

The Hyperledger Indy CLI will respond with:

```
Found claim Job-Certificate in connection Acme
Corp
Status: 2018-04-09 18:26:31.151414
Name: Job-Certificate
Version: 0.2
Attributes:
    first_name: Alice
    last_name: Garcia
    employee_status: Permanent
    experience: 3 years
    salary_bracket: between $50,000 to
$100,000
```

Now we see that Alice has everything needed for her to apply for a loan. The Loan will be provided by Thrift Bank. Connection details for Thrift Bank are provided within thrift-loan-application.indy file.

Let us look first into the thrift loan application request file by executing the show command:

```
ALICE@sandbox> show sample/thrift-loan-
application.indy
```

The Hyperledger Indy CLI will respond with the application content (which contains several proofs needed):

```
{
  "connection-request": {
```

```
    "name": "Thrift Bank",
    "identifier": "H2aKRiDeq8aLZSydQMDbtf",
    "nonce":
"77fbf9dc8c8e6acde33de98c6d747b28c",
    "endpoint": "124.34.56.189:7880"
  },
  "proof-requests": [{
      "name": "Loan-Application-Basic",
      "version": "0.1",
      "attributes": {
            "salary_bracket": "string",
            "employee_status": "string"
        },
        "verifiableAttributes":
["salary_bracket", "employee_status"]
    }, {
      "name": "Loan-Application-KYC",
      "version": "0.1",
      "attributes": {
            "first_name": "string",
            "last_name": "string",
            "ssn": "string"
        },
        "verifiableAttributes": ["first_name",
"last_name", "ssn"]
    }, {
      "name": "Name-Proof",
```

```
    "version": "0.1",
    "attributes": {
            "first_name": "string",
            "last_name": "string"
    },
    "verifiableAttributes": ["first_name",
"last_name"]
      }],
  "sig":
"D1vU5fbtJbqWKdCoVJgqHBLLhh5CYspikuEXdnBVVyCnL
HiYC9ZsZrDWpz3GkFFGvfC4RQ4kuB64vUFLo3F7Xk6"
}
```

Alice only needs a Basic Loan, she will only need to send her employment proof with the minimal personal information needed. We want to load the request from Thrift Bank firstly, so we will execute the load command in our terminal window:

```
ALICE@sandbox> load sample/thrift-loan-
application.indy
```

The Hyperledger Indy CLI will respond with request status:

```
1 connection request found for Thrift Bank.
Creating Connection for Thrift Bank.

Try Next:
    show connection "Thrift Bank"
    accept request from "Thrift Bank"
```

Now we will execute the accept command to accept the connection with Thrift Bank:

```
ALICE@sandbox> accept request from Thrift
```

The Hyperledger Indy CLI will respond with:

```
Expanding thrift to "Thrift Bank"
Request not yet verified.
Connection not yet synchronized.
Attempting to sync...

Synchronizing...
    Connection Thrift Bank synced
Accepting request with nonce
77fbf9dc8c8e6acde33de98c6d747b28c from id
NyvGP1B1RQ14wyUHAbVdNh
nLkB5S looking for Thrift Bank at
10.20.30.103:7777
nLkB5S pinged Thrift Bank at
HA(host='0.0.0.0', port=6002)
nLkB5S got pong from Thrift Bank

Signature accepted.

Response from Thrift Bank (1.59 ms):
    Trust established.
    DID created in Indy.
```

```
Synchronizing...
    Confirmed DID written to Indy.


Try Next:
    show proof request "Loan-Application-
Basic"
    send proof "Loan-Application-Basic" to
"Thrift Bank"
    show proof request "Loan-Application-KYC"
    send proof "Loan-Application-KYC" to
"Thrift Bank"
    show proof request "Name-Proof"
    send proof "Name-Proof" to "Thrift Bank"
```

Any organization can have different proof and claim types as supported within Hyperledger Indy Codebase.

Alice only wants a Basic Loan, so let us inspect the proof request for Basic Loan Application before we send any proofs. This is an important and reasonable step. Alice will do one more proof after the basic loan (which is know your customer – KYC proof). We can go back into the file content to understand but checking the single proof will always be faster. So, we will use the show command again to inspect the proof request by Thrift Bank:

```
ALICE@sandbox> show proof request Loan-
Application-Basic
```

The Hyperledger Indy CLI will respond with the proof details:

Found proof request "Loan-Application-Basic" in connection "Thrift Bank"

Status: Requested

Name: Loan-Application-Basic

Version: 0.1

Attributes:

    salary_bracket (V): between $50,000 to $100,000

    employee_status (V): Permanent

The Proof is constructed from the following claims:

    Claim (Job-Certificate v0.2 from Acme Corp)

            first_name: Alice

            last_name: Garcia

        * employee_status: Permanent

            experience: 3 years

        * salary_bracket: between $50,000 to $100,000

Try Next:

    set <attr-name> to <attr-value>

    send proof "Loan-Application-Basic" to "Thrift Bank"

The Basic Loan only requires a salary bracket and employment status. And it was automatically constructed from the Job certificate claim. Alice agrees on the data to be shared (which is now minimal) so she executes the send command to send the proof to Thrift Bank:

```
ALICE@sandbox> send proof Loan-Application-
Basic to Thrift Bank
```

The Ledger will respond (Via Hyperledger Indy CLI) with:

```
Signature accepted.
```

```
Response from Thrift Bank (479.17 ms):
    Your Proof Loan-Application-Basic 0.1 has
been received and verified
```

```
    Loan eligibility criteria satisfied,
please send another proof 'Loan-Application-
KYC'
```

Now Thrift Bank is asking Alice to submit Her KYC (Know Your Customer) application which will let the bank know her name and very basic information. Alice inspects the KYC Proof by executing the show command in the terminal:

```
ALICE@sandbox> show proof request Loan-
Application-KYC
```

The Hyperledger Indy CLI will respond with:

```
Found proof request "Loan-Application-KYC" in
connection "Thrift Bank"
```

```
Status: Requested
```

Name: Loan-Application-KYC

Version: 0.1

Attributes:

    [2] first_name (V): Alice
    [2] last_name (V): Garcia
    [1] ssn (V): 123-45-6789

The Proof is constructed from the following claims:

    Claim [1] (Transcript v1.2 from Faber College)

        student_name: Alice Garcia
    *   ssn: 123-45-6789
        degree: Bachelor of Science,
Marketing
        year: 2015
        status: graduated

    Claim [2] (Job-Certificate v0.2 from Acme Corp)

    *   first_name: Alice
    *   last_name: Garcia
        employee_status: Permanent
        experience: 3 years
        salary_bracket: between $50,000 to
$100,000

Try Next:

```
    set <attr-name> to <attr-value>
    send proof "Loan-Application-KYC" to
"Thrift Bank"
```

Hyperledger Indy Automatically filled the first name, last name and SSN bracket using the previous claims (Transcript and Job Certificate) for Alice. Everything Thrift Bank will about Alice now is:

1. Alice is Permanently Employed.
2. Alice's Salary ranges between 50,000 and 100,000 USD.
3. Alice's SSN is 123456789

Now Alice wants to send the KYC Proof so we will execute the send command in our terminal:

```
ALICE@sandbox> send proof Loan-Application-KYC
to Thrift Bank
```

The Thrift Bank will respond with:

```
Signature accepted.
```

```
Response from Thrift Bank (69.9 ms):
    Your Proof Loan-Application-KYC 0.1 has
been received and verified
```

We can expect that the remaining work can be accomplished in the real world, not behind a screen. This fictional story about

Alice (Thanks for the Hyperledger Community for this scenario and documentation) makes a good demonstration for protecting privacy using Blockchain Technology while providing trust to other entities such as ACME Corp.

Hyperledger Indy real world Development is surely more complicated than what we have seen in this quick tutorial. Developing Applications with Hyperledger Indy will require someone with Python background plus some passion to learn.

Hyperledger Indy Sub Projects

The Above tutorial mainly mentions Hyperledger Indy Node. which is the node development in a distributed ledger. Hyperledger Indy is the most important part of Hyperledger Indy and all other projects (except Hyperledger Indy SDK) are parts of it.

Hyperledger Indy Node is implemented based on Plenum. Plenum is a subproject of Hyperledger Indy too, but Hyperledger Indy Node extends its pool functionality to create a self-sovereign identity ecosystem.

To help clarify the image, Hyperledger Indy contains other four Dependent projects, and its repository consists of five (for Hyperledger Indy Node).

The Five Repository Parts are:

1- Code for Hyperledger Indy Client "indy-client".
2- Code for Hyperledger Indy Node "indy-node".
3- Shared code for both client and node "indy-common".
4- Scripts for installed nodes "scripts"
5- Scripts for Development setup "dev-setup".
6- documentation (which I do not count as actual code in my opinion).

While the four dependent projects (of Hyperledger Indy Node) are:

Indy Plenum

The code of the distributed ledger itself. Indy Plenum implements a Byzantine fault tolerance protocol like the one in Hyperledger Fabric. Plenum is built in Python and makes extensive use of threading management with async and await code keywords. Plenum uses libsodium cryptographic library, you will need to install this on your machine before starting development. The Consensus protocol used in Indy Plenum is RBFT Protocol; RBFT Protocol assumes one of the nodes connected to the network as a leader which determines the transactions order and communication between other nodes. other non-leading nodes are called "follower nodes". A Batch of transactions is committed after three phases of the consensus protocol.

Connected clients with appropriate permissions can send write requests (Transactions). while any other non-privileged node can only seek read requests. Therefore ACME Corp can issue a confirmation that Alice is their employee. while Thrift Bank can read this confirmation.

Once a node connects to the network, it makes a catchup request to another connected node to synchronize the ledger state with other nodes. maintaining a healthy blockchain state.

Indy AnonCreds

Implementation for anonymous credentials developed with Python initially by IBM Researchers.

Indy Anoncreds was built for exchanging proofs between sovereign identities in a Hyperledger Indy ecosystem by relying on a public key exchange without storing the claims and proofs itself on the ledger which protects the privacy of proofs and claims.

Hyperledger Indy AnonCreds will be suspended soon as its implementation will be moved to Indy SKD to make it easier to consume its features and provide a simpler architecture for the development process.

Indy SDK

This is the Software Development Kit for Hyperledger Indy. Indy SDK enables developers to build clients to consume Hyperledger Indy Anonymous and Private network. Indy SDK's base is the libindy library.

libindy is built in C Programming language as a C-Callable library that provides tools for building an application on top of Hyperledger Indy. libindy is available for popular desktop, mobile and server platforms. Additionally, you can use one of the following wrappers for libindy to consume Indy SDK in these programming languages:

1. Java; requires Java 8 or higher and can be installed easily with maven.
   Add this line to your repositories tag in pom.xml file:
   ```
   evernym
   https://repo.evernym.com/artifactory/libin
   dy-maven-local
   ```
   and add this line in your dependencies tag in pom.xml file:
   ```
   org.hyperledger indy 1.3.1-dev-410
   ```

2. Python; requires Python 3.6 or higher and can be installed easily with pip by executing:
   ```
   pip install python3-indy
   ```

3. Swift (iOS); can be installed with adding this line on top of your Pod File:

```
source
'https://github.com/hyperledger/indy-sdk.git'
```

then adding pod to build target with:
pod 'libindy-objc'
You will need some other prerequisites to work with iOS. they are:

   a. Rust and RustUp (visit rust-lang.org to download binaries).

   b. Toolchains; install it with this command:
```
rustup target add aarch64-apple-ios
armv7-apple-ios armv7s-apple-ios i386-apple-ios x86_64-apple-ios
```

   c. cargo-libo; install it with this command:
```
cargo install cargo-lipo
```

   d. libsodium; install it with this command:
```
brew install libsodium
```

   e. zeromq; install it with this command:
```
brew install zeromq
```

   f. cmake; If you don't already have it, install it with this command:
```
brew install cmake
```

Additionally, we will need to set some environment variables and build-libindy-core-ios.sh script file variables.

The Environment variables are:
```
export PKG_CONFIG_ALLOW_CROSS=1

export CARGO_INCREMENTAL=1
```
And the "build-libindy-core-ios.sh" file variables are:
```
export
OPENSSL_DIR=/usr/local/Cellar/openssl/1.0.
2k

export
EVERNYM_REPO_KEY=~/Documents/EvernymRepo

export LIBINDY_POD_VERSION=0.0.1
```

Please note that you must set OPENSSL_DIR path to your own installed OPENSSL library, EVERYNYM_REPO_KEY to a file path with a private key for authorization on deb server and LIBINDY_POD_VERSION to the current version of libindy-core pod you will be working with.

4. NodeJS; You will need C++ Build Tools and Python 2.7 Plus libindy 1.6 or higher in your system library path. For C++ build tools, depending on your platform you should have the following:

   a. For Linux: install any common C/C++ Compiler, and make.

   b. For macOS: install Command Line Tools from Xcode.

   c. For Windows: Install Visual Studio 2017 (Community Edition is free) and during the installation, make sure to select "Desktop Development with C++" option.
   Once installed, run the following command in an

elevated CMD or PowerShell:
npm config set msvs_version 2017

5. .NET; Just run "indy-sdk-dotnet-.sln" file which can be
   found under /wrappers/dot-net in the cloned repository.
   The project depends on several NuGet Packages. Search
   NuGet library if any of them is missing from your
   installation of Visual Studio.
   *Note: It's recommended to use Visual Studio 2017 or higher
   (Community Edition is enough).*

Hyperledger Indy SDK also includes Indy CLI. which is the
official command-line interface built specially to make it easier
for Developers & Network Operators to use Hyperledger Indy.

If you plan to make use of payment in your blockchain, then
you can use the included libnullpay which is packaged
alongside with Indy SDK.

Installing Hyperledger Indy SDK

Hyperledger Indy SDK has three versions:

1- master: this is a copy from the master branch of
   Hyperledger Indy SDK main repository.
2- rc: release candidates for new unofficial releases.
3- stable: the most recent stable release of Hyperledger
   Indy SDK.

Depending on your platform, follow these steps to install the
SDK:

1. Ubuntu: Use APT to install Indy SDK. Execute the
   following commands in your terminal:

```
sudo apt-key adv --keyserver
keyserver.ubuntu.com --recv-keys 68DB5E88

sudo add-apt-repository "deb
https://repo.sovrin.org/sdk/deb xenial
stable"

sudo apt-get update

sudo apt-get install -y libindy
```
Note: you can replace "stable" with whatever release version of Hyperledger Indy SDK you want to use.

2. Windows: visit "https://repo.sovrin.org/windows/libindy/stable" and download the stable (or rc/master). Unzip the archive to your desired directory and then add your directory to PATH environment variables.

3. macOS: Run the following commands with brew in your terminal to install libraries and tools required:
```
brew install pkg-config

brew install
https://raw.githubusercontent.com/Homebrew
/homebrew-
core/65effd2b617bade68a8a2c5b39e1c3089cc0e
945/Formula/libsodium.rb

brew install automake

brew install autoconf

brew install cmake

brew install openssl
```

```
brew install zeromq
```

```
brew install zmq
```

Then set up the following environment variables:

```
export PKG_CONFIG_ALLOW_CROSS=1
```

```
export CARGO_INCREMENTAL=1
```

```
export RUST_LOG=indy=trace
```

```
export RUST_TEST_THREADS=1
```

Then add a path variable for your OPENSSL Directory:
```
export
OPENSSL_DIR=/usr/local/Cellar/openssl/1.0.
2
```

Then clone the library to your local file system:

```
git clone
https://github.com/hyperledger/indy-
sdk.git
```

navigate to libindy folder with:

```
cd ./indy-sdk/libindy
```

and finally, use cargo to build the library with:

```
cargo build
```

Indy Crypto

This is a shared cryptographic library for all Hyperledger Indy Components. Built as a C-Callable library and based on both

Rust Lang and Apache Milagro Cryptographic Library (abbreviated AMCL).

Indy Crypto relies on the Boneh-Lynn-Shacham signature scheme (abbreviated BLS). BLS scheme uses a bilinear pairing to verify that the signer of a cryptographic object is authentic. BLS is proved to be strong even against theoretical random oracles.

Until the time of writing this book, Indy Crypto only provides wrappers for Python

Hyperledger Quilt And ILP

Hyperledger Quilt is here to allow connecting more than one ledger together using the Interledger Protocol (abbreviated ILP). Hyperledger Quilt is an implementation for the ILP written in Java as an organized Maven Project. Quilt is still yet new in my opinion (there are several open issues on GitHub) but developers are working to overcome this.

Interledger Protocol Overview

Interledger Protocol was originally invented by Ripple, the famous payment gateway behind the cryptocurrency which holds the same name. But now the Interledger W3C Community group is handling its development. There are more than 360 contributors in this group at the time of writing this book.

> Note: Interledger Protocol itself is not managed by Hyperledger Community, Hyperledger has its own implementation of the protocol which is Quilt.

There are main five design goals for the Interledger Protocol, they are:

1- Neutrality: Interledger Protocol itself shouldn't be tied to a specific company or network.

2- Interoperability: Interledger Protocol should be used between any two ledgers despite their types and technologies. even if these ledgers are not designed or built for interoperability.

3- Security: All Senders, receivers, and connectors should be protected and isolated from one another. connectors should not be able to steal money transferred (if any) from the senders or receivers. And Senders/Receivers should not be able to interfere in the operations of a connector.

4- Simplicity: Interledger Protocol Core should be simple as much as possible Because simplification minimizes the requirements for agreements between ledgers connecting through Interledger Protocol.

5- End-to-End Principle: Any feature that is not needed in the core Interledger Protocol itself should be moved to the edges of the network (the sender and receiver ledgers). This serves to keep the ledger as simple as possible and move responsibility for non-core features to ledgers where these responsibilities belong originally.

To Simplify Interledger Protocol flow let us go through a simple packet lifecycle. Assuming a sender and receiver through an account. an **account** here is an established connection between two peers to track obligations between them. We also assume that both sender and receiver have digital funds on a shared ledger system; Here is what will happen:

1. Sender starts an ILP PREPARE packet with the account, conditions, amount and expiry as parameters. any additional data can be also included. The PREPARE packet must be sent through an authenticated and secured communication channel.

2. Connector will receive the packet. determines which account to be debited based on the communication channel it has received the packet from (each account has its own communication channel).

3. Connector will check if the sender has enough credit to send the specified amount of money to the receiver.

   a. If yes, then the connector will deduct the amount from the sender account.

   b. If no, the connector will reply to the Sender with REJECT packet.

4. The connector will use its local routing table to find the next hop to send the message to. The next hop might be another connector or the final receiver. The next hop will handle the first connector as a sender. meaning that the new connector (or final receiver) will deduct the amount from the old connector as the old connector did with the original sender.

5. Step 4 is repeated until the packet gets to the final receiver.

6. The final receiver will check the PREPARE Packet. To accept the packet, the receiver will send a FULFILL packet. containing a preimage of the condition in the PREPARE packet. the FULFULL packet will go all the

way back to the original sender. If the receiver does not wish to accept the packet, it can send a REJECT packet instead that will go all the way back alongside the amount until it reaches the original sender.

7. the sender will check the preimage of the FULFILL Packet to make sure it matches the condition it originally sent. The Sender is permitted to keep a local copy of the transaction stored on their side.

Requirements for Hyperledger Quilt

Hyperledger Quilt is built in Java and depends on Java Cryptographic Extension (abbreviated JCE).

JCE is not packaged within normal JDK. It must be downloaded from Oracle Website and installed locally on the machine. Visit "https://www.oracle.com/technetwork/java/javase/downloads/jce8-download-2133166.html" to download.

Hyperledger Quilt uses Maven to manage dependencies, for your repositories section, paste the following code snippet:

```
<repository>
    <id>sonatype</id>

<url>https://oss.sonatype.org/content/repositories/snapshots/</url>
    </repository>
```

And in your dependencies section, add the following:

```
<dependency>
    <groupId>org.interledger</groupId>
```

```
    <artifactId>java-ilp-core</artifactId>
    <version>0.13.0-SNAPSHOT</version>
</dependency>
```

You can now proceed to build with maven normally by executing:

```
mvn clean install
```

in the root folder of your project where Hyperledger Quilt libraries were included.

You can also use Gradle to import libraries, add the Snapshot repository to your Gradle properties file.

```
repositories {
    mavenCentral()
    maven {
        url
"https://oss.sonatype.org/content/repositories
/snapshots/"
    }
}
```

and for dependencies, add the following line:

```
compile group: 'org.interledger', name: 'java-
ilp-core', version: '0.13.0-SNAPSHOT'
```

And then you can proceed to build your project normally.

Here is a code snippet for sending a Packet programmatically (the very same packet we have discussed as a sample for packet lifecycle)

```
InterledgerPreparePacket
interledgerPreparePacket =
  InterledgerPreparePacket.builder()
    .destination(destination)
    .amount(amount)
    .executionCondition(condition)
    .expiresAt(expiry)
    .data(data)
    .build();
```

The Documentation for Hyperledger Quilt is not yet completed. the project is in version 0.1.3. A bit of exploration spirit is needed with its functions, or you can always open an issue on GitHub Repository.

Hyperledger Caliper in Action

Hyperledger Caliper is a blockchain benchmarking tool. The main goal is to allow developers to test blockchain they've developed in order to check its capabilities.

Hyperledger Caliper – at the time of writing this book – supports three blockchain solutions, they are:

1- Hyperledger Fabric 1.0 or higher.
2- Hyperledger Sawtooth 1.0 or higher
3- Hyperledger Iroha 1.0 beta 3 or higher.

Integrations for Other Blockchain frameworks are now under development. Integration with Hyperledger Composer is also supported to maintain easier benchmarking execution.

There are four supported indicators within Hyperledger Caliper, they are:

1- Success Rate
2- Transaction/Read Throughput
3- Transaction/Read Latency (Minimum, Maximum, Average, Percentile).
4- Resource Consumption (CPU, Memory, Network IO and other resources).

Some Perquisites are required before building Hyperledger Caliper, they are:

1- NodeJS 8.0 or higher.

2- Node-GYP

3- Docker

4- Docker Compose

Clone the Hyperledger Caliper repository from GitHub, in your command-line interface, execute:

```
git clone
https://github.com/hyperledger/caliper.git
```

Once cloned, install dependencies locally by executing:

```
npm install
```

The next step will be to install the proper blockchain SDKs for the blockchain framework in which your application is developed.

For Hyperledger Fabric, run the following command in the root folder for the cloned folder:

```
npm install grpc@1.10.1 fabric-ca-client@1.1.0
fabric-client@1.1.0
```

In this command, replace the 1.1.0 with your current version of Hyperledger Fabric. The 1.10.1 is the version of grpc itself and it is not related to the version of Hyperledger Fabric you are using.

For Hyperledger Sawtooth, run the following command to install dependencies in the root folder.

```
npm install protocol-buffers
```

then install Hyperledger Sawtooth SDK by executing:

```
npm install sawtooth-sdk
```

For Hyperledger Iroha, you will need to install Iroha lib by executing the following command in the root folder:

```
npm install --no-save iroha-lib@0.1.7
```

The Hyperledger Iroha lib for Caliper is still an alpha version. meaning that you might encounter some issues with it. You can find a list of issues by visiting the issues section on the Hyperledger Iroha GitHub repository. If your issue is unique – which is uncommon – you can always open a new issue and the Hyperledger Iroha maintainers team will help you.

Running Benchmarks

You can find all predefined benchmarks in the benchmark folder in the folder of your cloned repository.

There are several benchmarks available there to be used, including a subfolder for a benchmark called "Small Bank" Where you can test transactions on a small simulation of a decentralized bank with user accounts and money transfers.

We will go through the "simple" benchmark subfolder to try out some basic benchmarks.

The folder contains the following:

1- configuration files for:

    a. Hyperledger Fabric

    b. Hyperledger Iroha

    c. Hyperledger Sawtooth

    d. ZooKeeper (this is for benchmarking with multiple clients in action)

2- Configuration file for the benchmark itself (main.js).

3- definitions for already provided sample Hyperledger Fabric, Iroha and Sawtooth networks.

To run the first benchmark, execute the following command in your terminal:

```
node benchmark/simple/main.js -c
yourconfig.json -n yournetwork.json
```

The -c parameter specifies the configuration for your test, if this is not provided then the default config.json file will be used. You should replace it with the proper file for your network (if not customized) from the simple benchmark folder. For example, if your network is a Hyperledger Fabric Network then you should use the "fabric-config.json" file from the simple benchmark folder.

The -n parameter specifies the configuration for your network itself. if not specified the benchmark will fail unless its address is provided within the first config file itself. If you're using Iroha, Sawtooth or Fabric sample networks then you can use the network definition packaged in the "simple" subfolder. You will find files named "iroha.json", "fabric.json" and "iroha.json".

We will use Hyperledger Fabric basic network - which we have described earlier in Fabric Deep Dive Section of this book – as samples for benchmarking commands. If you are running a different network then you should consider replacing configuration file names and paths with proper configuration files for your own network.

Proceeding with Hyperledger Fabric Network being benchmarked, the command should be:

```
node benchmark/simple/main.js -c fabric-
config.json -n fabric.json
```

Giving a quick look at the "config-fabric.json" file. we can see – near the file beginning - the following command object with both start and end commands:

```
"command" : {
    "start": "docker-compose -f
network/fabric/simplenetwork/docker-
compose.yaml up -d",
    "end" : "docker-compose -f
network/fabric/simplenetwork/docker-
compose.yaml down;docker rm $(docker ps -
aq);docker rmi $(docker images dev* -q)"
}
```

The start command is the command executed before benchmarking occurs. The default command here loads the docker compose for the selected network.

The end command is the command executed after the benchmarking complete. The default command takes docker compose down.

You can create a copy of the "config-fabric.json" file. add your own commands to happen before and after benchmarking to maintain your customized network – if any – needed commands for a more realistic benchmarking.

If we go a bit down in the same file, we can see a rounds test configuration JSON object. containing definition for clients, their type and their count. By Default, you will get a test configuration like this:

```
"test": {
    "clients": {
        "type": "local",
        "number": 5
}
```

This configuration indicates that the benchmarking will start five local clients for testing your blockchain network. You can set this number to whichever number of clients you want. Just keep your machine computational power in mind.

It is also possible to run benchmark through npm run command which will show automatically all available benchmarks you can use.

By executing the "npm run list" command in the root directory of cloned repository, you should see an output similar to this:

```
> caliper@0.1.0 list /home/hurf/caliper
> node ./scripts/list.js
Available benchmarks:
drm
simple
```

Indicating the available benchmarks for your network. As the "list.js" file returns a dynamically generated list of available benchmarks for your network.

To run a specific test from the above menu, your command will not be much different than the first method. execute the following command in your terminal for testing fabric network with a simple test:

```
npm test -- simple -c
./benchmark/simple/config.json -n
./benchmark/simple/fabric.json
```

You should see a detailed log on your terminal starting with output similar to:

```
> caliper@0.1.0 test /home/hurf/caliper
```

```
> node ./scripts/test.js "simple" "-c"
"./benchmark/simple/config.json" "-n"
"./benchmark/simple/fabric.json"
```

In both cases, either if you are using npm or not; a report file for your benchmark will be saved into the root directory in HTML format once the benchmark has been completed.

Benchmarking with Distributed clients and ZooKeeper

Another method for benchmarking is to use ZooKeeper – which is supported within Hyperledger Caliper – to benchmark the blockchain network with multiple clients from within multiple hosts. This is a closer step to maintain realistic feedback on blockchain network performance.

To run such a benchmark, make sure that the ZooKeeper service is installed on your machine. Plus, synchronizing time between machines (As any Blockchain consuming app would do) before moving on.

Then we will need to:

Firstly, Start The ZooKeeper Service.

Secondly, Launch clients on each target machine by executing:

```
node ./src/comm/client/zoo-client.js
zookeeper-server
```
Or
```
npm run startclient -- zookeeper-server
```

on this step, you should get an output similar to the following should be displayed in terminal:

```
caliper@0.1.0 startclient /home/hyperledger-
mc/caliper
node ./src/comm/client/zoo-client.js
"10.201.33.14.5412"
Connected to ZooKeeper
Created client
node:/caliper/clients/client_1524478952443_000
0000003
Created receiving queue
at:/caliper/client_1524478952443_0000000003_in
Created sending queue
at:/caliper/client_1524478952443_0000000003_ou
t
Waiting for messages
at:/caliper/client_1524478952443_0000000003_in
......
```

You will need to set client settings in the configuration file to zookeeper, your configuration file clients section should look something similar to:

```
"clients": {
  "type": "zookeeper",
  "zoo" : {
    "server": "10.201.33.14.5412",
    "clientsPerHost": 5
  }
}
```

Finally, start the benchmark on any machine as we did before while testing on a single machine. The output HTML file will contain a detailed benchmark report.

The Repository contains another subfolder for documentation that is updated with every release. documentation is written in md format. meaning that the best way to read them is through the GitHub Repository web page.

Repository documentation contains architecture and design-specific information that are useful if you are willing to provide support for Hyperledger Caliper to benchmark any other blockchain network other than those already supported.

One last thing!

I want to give you a **one-in-two-hundred chance** to win a **$200.00 Amazon Gift card** as a thank-you for reading this book.

All I ask is that you give me some feedback, so I can improve this or my next book :)

Your opinion is *super valuable* to me. It will only take a minute of your time to let me know what you like and what you didn't like about this book. The hardest part is deciding how to spend the two hundred dollars! Just follow this link.

http://reviewers.win/hyperledger

www.ingramcontent.com/pod-product-compliance
Lightning Source LLC
Chambersburg PA
CBHW060532060326
40690CB00017B/3468